"INTO THE BAY—THE GREAT, WIDE, WEALTH-FRINGED BAY."

CITY LEGENDS

BY
WILL CARLETON
AUTHOR OF
"FARM BALLADS" "FARM LEGENDS" "CITY BALLADS"
"FARM FESTIVALS" ETC., ETC.

ILLUSTRATED

NEW YORK
HARPER & BROTHERS, FRANKLIN SQUARE

Copyright, 1889, by HARPER & BROTHERS.

All rights reserved.

Dedicated

TO THE MEMORY OF

"JUDDIE"

Preface.

IT will be noticed that these Legends are divided into seven different Chains. Whether the links of dialogue and interlude with which they are connected be gold, silver, or base metal, the author will not say—he really does not pretend to know. Whether the pendants of poems that hang from them be diamonds, pearls, rubies, or worthless paste, how can he guarantee? Literary jewelry (if poetry may be so called) depends largely for its value upon the eyes that gaze upon it, and the hearts that wear it.

The real preface to this book is formed by those which have preceded it from the same author; a like purpose actuates them all. But he takes another opportunity to thank his large family of readers for their continued faithfulness and loyalty, and to assure them that he is still laboring to deserve their respect and affection.

C.

Contents.

First Chain—*Including*,

	PAGE
DIALOGUES	15
LEGEND SONG	16
THE SANDAL-MAKER OF BABYLON	19
FARMER STEBBINS TOBOGGANS	24
DIOGENES'S DAUGHTER	30
FARMER STEBBINS AT THE BAT	36
DIONYSIUS'S MIRROR	41
UNCLE NATE'S FUNERAL	44

Second Chain—*Including*,

DIALOGUES	51
THE HERO OF THE TOWER	56
TRUE TO BROTHER SPEAR	62
TWELVE O'CLOCK	66

Third Chain—*Including*,

DIALOGUES	79
HYMN OF THANKSGIVING	82
THE VOICE OF A STAR	83
THE OLD HYMN-BOOK	86
THE PASTOR'S FAREWELL	88
THE CONVICT'S CHRISTMAS EVE	93

Fourth Chain—*Including,*

	PAGE
PRELUDES	103
THE CAPTAIN IS ASLEEP	104
THE VESTAL	109
SONG OF THE UNBUILT SHIP	110
THE SERPENT OF THE STILL	114

Fifth Chain—*Including,*

DIALOGUES	121
THE NEGRO FUNERAL	122
THE FOUR TRAVELLERS	127
THE EARTHQUAKE PRAYER	129

Sixth Chain.—*Historical Drama.*

SCENE I.—BENEDICT ARNOLD AT QUEBEC	137
SCENE II.—AT PHILADELPHIA	141
SCENE III.—NEAR LONDON	144

Seventh Chain—*Including,*

DIALOGUES	153
KIDNAPPED IN MERCY	159
LADY BOUNTIFUL'S TRIUMPH	166

Illustrations.

	PAGE
"Into the bay—the great, wide, wealth-fringed bay"	*Frontispiece.*
".... The king, with a humorous sense, requested of him an audience"	21
"With sober face, but eyes upon the broadest kind of grin"	27
"Sir, I am your daughter, if you please"	33
"Produced an unforeseen result"	39
"And they have scampered far and near, and picked the freshest flowers"	45
True to Brother Spear	63–65
".... A form—or was he dreaming?"	71
"And o'er their shoulders his arms he threw"	91
"An open church some look of welcome wore"	95
"Tender words of him are said"	105
"A wreck that has ne'er been sailed"	111
"He twines about her trembling life"	115
And he said: "Now don' be weepin' for dis pretty bit o' clay"	123
"But there sudden rose among them one of earth's untutored kings"	131
".... Will you reap this field of glory?"	139
"I have no friend in earth, or heaven, or hell!"	147
"There's many a green little grass-mound"	157
"He stays at our house nights"	161

FIRST CHAIN.

CITY LEGENDS.

First Chain.

SCENE, *a Farm-house Parlor. Various delegates from six families are present. Storm-concert out in the darkness, and waves of snow drifting against the east windows. Large fireplace, full of forest-logs, gradually turning to flame-colored gold.*

EDITH (*a blue-eyed girl*).
'Tis Legend-night; and all our club are here,
Except the new school-master: who will come
A little later.
    ISABEL (*a black-eyed girl*).
                For he told you so?
    EDITH (*primly*).
He told us all so. While we wait for him,
He said we should not merely wait, but work,
And sing the Legend Song in our best style.
    HARRY (*a tall young man*).
The one he taught you?
    EDITH (*tartly*).
                One he taught us all.
He shows no partiality in school.
                    [*Quiet, incredulous laughter.*
    DAVID (*a short, fat young man*).
Allow me, Edith, since he is not here,
To lead you to the organ fearlessly.
                [*Ripples of restrained laughter. All sing.*

LEGEND SONG.

I.

Dreamy legends of the past,
    Sombre-hued or pleasant,
Though by sun or cloud o'ercast,
    Plain you show the present!
And the future you can see,
For what was again shall be;
Shadows far ahead you cast,
Dreamy legends of the past!

II.

Stirring legends of to-day,
    Draped in modern dresses,
How you light the darksome way
    Of the past recesses!
Showing, as the age goes on,
What men were in days agone;
For, with inconsistence strange,
Times may change, but never change.

A knock at the outer door. Enter SCHOOL-MASTER, *well covered with snow. All spring to meet him except* EDITH, *who remains at the organ, studying the music.*

SCHOOL-MASTER (*to the others, after glancing at* EDITH).
Well, here I come; still in the human form,
Half-victim of a nineteenth century blizzard;
Yet wholly pleased; because you have agreed
That one night in the week you will devote
To legends of the present and the past,
Dropping those games, whose names I now forget—
    DAVID (*the fat young man, eagerly*).
Snap up and catch 'em, Charley can't catch me,
Green grow the rushes, Oats peas beans and barley,
Threading the needle, Jack-straws, Blind-Man's-Buff,
Going to Rome—
    All the girls.
        Enough! enough! the Legends!

Enter some OLDER PEOPLE, *timidly, and are given chairs by* MABEL, *a brown-eyed girl, and others.*

    One of the OLDER PEOPLE.
Are we admitted to the company?
    SCHOOL-MASTER.
This is a game that every age can play.
Now first let us go back to ancient times:
To some of those old cities of the past;
Those killed and buried cities of the past,
And yet which live, as truly now as then.
    Squire STOUT (*a florid, middle-aged man*).
I've seen the pictures of them ruined towns,
But noticed nothin' much, excep', perhaps,
Some stone-piles, ditches, heaps of earth, an' things
That looked like broken steeples out o' churches.
    SCHOOL-MASTER.
And yet they live—those cities of the past:
They were not burned—nor were they beaten down
By the iron shoes of conquest; lightning broke
From its black floating jail of clouds, and dealt
Hot, glistening blows upon them; earthquakes came,
And shook them by the throat; tornadoes rushed
In loud, swift journeys through the staggering streets,
And crowded them with coffins; rot and sloth,
Corruption, Hate, Greed, War, and blear-eyed Lust
Have been disastrous citizens; until
The cities seemed to sink, corpse-like, in earth.
And yet they live, old cities of the past.
    Squire STOUT.
I s'pose perhaps that's true; it sounds like print;
But I don't seem to catch the meaning on't.
    SCHOOL-MASTER.
Those walls and domes their people blindly built,
Were naught except thin shells, round city-souls;
The mounds where we for treasures grope and search,
Are cemeteries, holding their crushed bones.
Two forms have all things; that which can not live,
And that which can not die.

Squire STOUT.
                       Too deep for me.
    SCHOOL-MASTER.
They live in many worlds. On History's plains,
Their towers still camp beneath the bright-eyed sun.
The student's lamp illumes their sombre streets,
The architect is measuring up their walls,
The merchant knows the tonnage of their ships,
The history-general fights their battles o'er,
The theologian trims their temple-fires,
And delves among their creeds, both false and true;
    Squire STOUT (*aside*).
We did not hire the teacher, I'll be bound,
To go round nights, and spout such stuff as this.
    SCHOOL-MASTER (*continuing*).
They live among the hills of poesy.
The artist throws their ancient colors on
The hungry regions of his canvas page;
The weird romancer, with sharp-pointed pen
That pricks the veins of human nature dry,
Has brought them, in Imagination's ships,
Real men and women, gathered from all lands
And times—and mingled by his wizard touch.
The poet says that fancy, love, and hate,
With kiss of velvet or with tread of iron,
Once walked the pavement of those minds and hearts.
    Squire STOUT (*aside*).
Oh, poetry be hanged! it never ploughed
A field, or mowed an acre of marsh-grass.
    SCHOOL-MASTER (*continuing*).
Perhaps they are in Future-land; where those
Who lived in them a while, now live for aye.
Perchance, among their memory-household wares,
They bore away mind-pictures of the towns—
The old half-loved, half-hated towns of earth.
Do they not often build, in that long dream—
So vivid that it makes this fleet-paced life
But half remembered—seem itself a dream—
The cherished walls and towers of ancient times?

Exiles from home, they drag home after them;
And in their memory, the old cities live.
    Squire STOUT (*aside, yawning*).
I'd drag myself home, if it wasn't so cold.
    SCHOOL-MASTER (*continuing*).
Now tell us tales, old cities of the past!
Give us some stories of your short earth-life!
Tell us some ancient legends, that may be
Both like and unlike to the present days.
Furnish some useful lesson, that The Past—
That famed professor of all sciences—
May teach us, from his century-woven chair!
Forth from the heaped-up mounds that mark the throne
Where that great city-king called Babylon
Reigned for a thousand years—a spectre walks,
Telling us many legends of old times;
And one of them breathes nineteenth-century air,
Aided by one of us, who'll voice his story.
    HARRY (*the tall young man*) *reads:*

THE SANDAL-MAKER OF BABYLON.

He was rather a picturesque old man, upon a pettily complex plan,
With grim ability, never hid, to superintend what others did,
And state — an effort's race being run — how things that were done
    should have been done.
Naught e'er was made but he could tell how he could have made
    it twice as well;
Naught e'er destroyed but he would bet that he could have smashed
    it finer yet.
And this erratum of mankind sat, all day, a moral and mental cat,
And threw the claws of his intellect at every merit and defect,
And into the palace and the cot, and into what men were and were not,
And into the deeds they struggled through, and into the things they
    failed to do,
Using the most uncalled-for cares with other people and their affairs,
And viewed, with a supercilious smile, the work of the world; and
    made, meanwhile,
The poorest sandals under the sun—the sandal-maker of Babylon.

No one was ever, since earth began, religious enough to please this
 man;
No one to the gods e'er bowed a knee, that could have done it as
 low as he;
The tower of Belus itself, he thought, if men had builded it as they
 ought,
Had been much pleasanter to the eye, and several hundred times as
 high.
He knew just how it came to pass that Nebuchadnezzar was fed
 with grass;
Could he have only had his way, the monarch's feed should have
 been of hay.
In fact, no person, high or low, had fault to conceal or merit to
 show,
But he could figure it to a notch, and hold it up for the world to
 watch.
And yet, withal, his moral gait was that of a deep old reprobate,
Full of fool-actions shrewdly done—the sandal-maker of Babylon.

No man was better able to tell how dead men might be living and
 well.
He knew the parts of the human frame, and every organ he called
 by name;
A theory of his own had he that man wasn't made as he ought to
 be;
Could have creation by him been done, the job would have been a
 better one:
No ill to mankind ever came but he had remedies for the same,
But never a word about them said until the suffering man was dead,
And yet, in spite of his mental wealth, he never had any kind of
 health;
The sickliest creature under the sun was the sandal-maker of Babylon.

You'd think, to hear him talk, that he invented money itself. He'd
 see
The gone-by chances of every trade—how every bargain should *have*
 been made;
He'd tell the rich why they were so; the poor, why they were not;
 could show

"..... THE KING, WITH A HUMOROUS SENSE, REQUESTED OF HIM AN AUDIENCE."

How even the king's great national purse might have been managed
    better or worse;
Yet had he one financial lack: he might be kicked to Susa and back,
And not a coin of any shape from his habiliments would escape:
Wealth always had contrived to shun the sandal-maker of Babylon.

But he began, unlucky elf, at criticising the king himself;
And so his head, as one might say, endangered even itself one day;
For soon the king, with a humorous sense, requested of him an audience;
And said, "I have heard you can not live beneath such government
    as I give:
There's no necessity for the same, and no one but ourselves to
    blame.
So, sage of the lapstone, do not grieve: I will give you every chance
    to leave;
This gallows you shall be hanged upon, O sandal-maker of Babylon."

The engine of death the old man scanned, and murmured, in accents
    soft and bland,
"Well, hang, if it does you any good; but I want it expressly understood
That were this gallows made by me, a deadlier weapon it would be.
I go to the other world; no doubt things over there need straightening
    out."

The monarch laughed, and lightly said, "You'd be a nuisance, alive
    or dead.
Go back to your stall and pound away, and think your thinkings
    and say your say."
"A foolish plan you have hit upon," said the sandal-maker of Babylon

And never again the old man stayed one happy day at his double
    trade;
"I do not like to retain my head by anybody's permit," he said.
"If king were I and I the king, I couldn't have spared him for anything."
And slow and surely, day by day, he lost his vigor and pined away;
They found him lying dead alone—sad sandal-maker of Babylon.

And even now throughout this earth (I tell the story for what 'tis worth)
They say his restless spirit runs, and makes its home with various ones.
Few families are so happy they have not a visit from him some day;
Few towns so blessed with fortune's smile that he doesn't live there
    for a while;
He will find fault till earth is done—crank sandal-maker of Babylon.

    Grandfather BELL (*a tall, straight, well-aged gentleman*).
Just like the old school-master George X. Jones
Down at the Corners.
    Elder STARR (*a large man of middle age*).
Just like Old Deacon Growlett, in our church.
    Miss PRYDE (*a tall, bright-eyed spinster*).
Just like old Miss Bakérre, the milliner.
    SCHOOL-MASTER (*aside*).
Just like my school director.
    [*Aloud*]   We come now
(Since contrasts often light each other up)
To present times, and one who lives to-day;
Whose nature is as clear as summer skies,
And simple as a baby's; but whose nerves
So tremble with ambition, that he jumps
From one scrape to another.—We will have
Read by Miss Mabel's clear and flute-like voice,
    EDITH (*aside*).
Miss Mabel's clear and flute-like voice, indeed.
    SCHOOL-MASTER (*continuing*).
A letter from our good and cumbrous friend,
Old Farmer Stebbins; telling his mishaps
In dealing with that modern city craze,
The swift toboggan slide.
    MABEL *reads:*

FARMER STEBBINS TOBOGGANS.

DEAR COUSIN JOHN: ROCHESTER, *February* 28.
    I got here safe, uncommonly alone,
      An' walked the streets in head-up style quite willin' to be known;
    With all the triumph in my eyes of one who works an' waits,
      An' in my overcoat a pair of first-class roller skates;

First Chain.

An', anxious out of glory's well a bucketful to drink,
I never stopped until I reached that same old skating rink.

For ever since the fearful night* I wrote about before,
I've swathed up safe an' practised sly upon my granary floor;
I tumbled till it sagged the joists, but persevered an' beat,
An' skated like a critter born with casters on its feet;
An' now I says, "These swells will learn — what my best neighbors know—
That, when he all unwinds himself, Old Stebbins ain't so slow."

But when I reached that festive place, 'twas locked up, I declare,
An' everything was desolate like, an' not a soul was there!
While on the door a brand-new sign said: "Stand up for the Right!
Salvation Army holds this fort! Prayer-meeting every night!"
I asked where all the skaters was; a passin' boy replied,
"Rink's bu'st; they're all a-takin' in the new toboggan slide!"

"Ah me!" I said; "the same old game! It's 'one go all go sheep!'"
Then started off to find the place as fast as I could creep;
For, though I criticise my race, I can't help but belong;
An' soon I found myself within the same old giddy throng.
But now they played at down an' up, instead of roun' an' roun',
An' skated somewhat like I did the night that I fell down.

An' some was dressed in usual style—the same as any one—
An' some had nightcaps, red an' blue, an' small bed-blankets on;
An' some rode head-first on their chins, an' some sat stiff an' still,
An' 'twasn't unlike the good old times we used to ride down-hill.
(But all through life I've noticed, 'mongst girls, women, boys, an' men—
This climbin' up to some large height, to be pushed down again!)

As I thus mused, who should come up the easy, stair-cased slopes,
But my old young true treacherous friend Miss Is'bel Sunnyhopes!

---

* Referring to his troubles in the skating rink, detailed in "City Ballads," where may also be found others of Farmer Stebbins' adventures.

Who's got me into more small scrapes than any girl on earth,
An' always helped me out again, with tender-seasoned mirth;
But everything looked safe like as she fluttered to my side,
And said, "My dear friend!—is it you?—do come and have a slide!"

She borrowed from a smart young man—a fellow that she knew—
A han'-sled with the runners gone—just big enough for two;
They'd rode in partnership, it seems; an' he gave up his place,
With something that wasn't quite content upon his lengthenin' face;
An' off we flew, with speed that shocked an' made me almost blind,
Fast as that first tobogganer—the foeman of mankind.

We went straight down, an' clim back safe; an' no mishap had known,
If I had heard cold Reason say, "Let well enough alone."
But Isabel's young fellow looked as sour as sour could be,
An' just as if he'd like to make a mince-pie out of me;
An' so I says, "I'll lengthen still this young man's underlip,"
And turned to Isabel an' said, "Let's take another trip."

The second ride I gave a glance at two small boards that lay
On edge, to keep us sliders in the straight an' narrow way;
My eyes was sort of misted like, I lost or lent my head,
An' grabbed these boards, supposin' them a portion of the sled;
I stopped off; an' the sleigh went on; an' left me, in a trice,
A-hangin' there with nothin' much betwixt me an' the ice.

"Hold on!" "Let go!" "Climb up!" "Slide down!" I heard the people roar:
I didn't know which one not to do, an' so I tried all four.
I kicked an' grabbed an' clim an' clawed, an' felt from foot to scalp
As if I was in Switzerland a-hangin' to an Alp;
My skates hopped out an' skittered off like boys let clear of school
(First time they'd ever run without an old bald-headed fool)!

My hat an' specs skipped clean away, as if they'd caught the craze,
An' been a-longin' for this chance for several nights and days;
Three apples an' five doughnuts, an' a purchased bakery bun,
All tried the new toboggan slide, an' went down, one by one;

"WITH SOBER FACE, BUT EYES UPON THE BROADEST KIND OF GRIN."

An' as for me—as some girls say, in that "brook" song they sing,
I "slipped an' slid an' gloomed an' glanced," an' grabbed at every-
    thing.

An' finally I twisted round, head-foremost, on my back,
An' went down like a lightnin' train that's just run off the track,
An' reached the bottom of the hill within a little while,
Then rolled an' scooted somethin' like a quarter of a mile;
An' when I gathered up, unhurt, but awful unattired,
I felt some like the waddin' of a shot-gun lately fired.

Then Isabel came softly up, with Pity's soothin' charms,
An' all of my lost property scooped in her han'some arms,
An' re'lly hoped I wasn't hurt—and handed me a pin—
With sober face, but eyes upon the broadest kind of grin;
And then her fellow came, and made a show of helpin' me;
But that 'ere underlip of his was short as short could be.

An' then I turned, an' said "Good-by" to all the people round;
"My friends, I'm out of place again; on more than slippery ground!
This goin' back upon their age is what no one should do;
It's hard to play the fine young man an' be an old one too.
Farewell to rinks an' slides while days aroun' me slip an' roll!
I'll spend the spare time after this on my immortal soul."

  DAVID (*the short, fat young man*).
I'd like to know that Is'bel Sunnyhopes:
I'll bet she's "up to snuff."
  ISABEL (*the black-eyed girl*), *aside, sniffing, half scornfully.*
      Yes, just about.
  Mr. ILLS (*an obese, elderly gentleman*).
This Mr. Stebbins, I should calculate,
Is just like old Jim Gosport, on the hill.
  Mrs. ILLS (*aside*).
He's just like you.
  SCHOOL-MASTER.
     Now we again will go
Back till we reach the temple-guarded hills
Of ancient Greece: Miss Edith here has found

A legend of that old philosopher
Diogenes, which she will read to us.
　　Edith (*aside*).
Though not in Mabel's clear and flute-like voice.
　　Reads:

DIOGENES'S DAUGHTER.

There is a legend that Diogenes,
　　Old pachyderm, once, basking in the sun,
Scolding the lazy, lying at his ease,
　　And peddling wisdom-loaflets underdone,
Saw suddenly a fair-haired maiden pass;
　　And, his digestion being good that day,
He took a new, strange fancy to the lass,
　　And even followed her a little way,
And asked her heart; which she, with mind obtuse,
Gave over to him, like a little goose.

For even his grimness had a fascination;
　　And, though no ladies' man, yet he could fire
The average female heart with admiration,
　　Being so unlike what they *should* admire.
And he had strong brain, and could "govern men,"
　　And hence win women; and she had a pride
To draw the crank old bachelor from his den,
　　And be known as a famous person's bride;
Besides, good women's hearts will often move
With love for men they do not half approve.

Whether she lived, there is no need to ask;
　　For he was soon a beastlier beast than ever,
And growled at her full many a tasteless task,
　　Beyond a woman's possible endeavor.
He wanted her to share his tub with him;
　　To carry lanterns for him through the street,
When, with dishonest eyes by pride made dim,
　　He strove the unknown Honest Man to meet;
And to agree, when that same man was found,
To look the other way or on the ground;—

First Chain.

She died, and he, in first-class cynic style,
    Forgot her, with serene self-contemplation,
Frowned at the world through his sardonic smile,
    And went on making rules for all creation;
Forgot the sweet girl baby that his wife
    Coaxed out of heaven and left on earth for him;
And strangers had to feed her simple life,
    While he went on, keeping the world in trim.
(He's not the last man who, to wail and preach,
Has left his children in the devil's reach.)

But she grew, good and pure; and as a child
    Felt strangely drawn unto the strange old man
Who walked the streets like to a brute half wild,
    Or sat majestic while his mean tongue ran;
But when she was eighteen she learned the truth;
    And walked up to him with half-awkward ease,
And with the blushing bashfulness of youth
    Said, "Sir, I am your daughter, if you please."
And, his digestion being good that day,
He let the pretty girl lead him away.

She took him to her home—a fairy bower—
    She petted him, she groomed his crazy hair,
She ruled him with her weak and tender power,
    She soothed out his belligerent despair;
She brought real feeling to his numb old heart,
    She charmed him with her sweet and winsome glee,
She gently pried his mental shell apart,
    And grasped the pearls that gave him agony;
While her friends said, "Just teach him common-sense,
And we'll be glad to stand the whole expense."

She made him see that life was something more
    Than crouching like a beast beneath the sun;
He came to praise the dainty robes she wore,
    And have some care what he himself put on;
He saw that honest goods, instead of pelf,
    Were symbols bright of industry and power;

That there was something else besides one's self
    To fill the minutes of life's quick-spent hour;
She made the sage less picturesque and keen,
But several times as happy and as clean.

And he was coming very fast to be
    A loving father—full of thrift's strong charm;
Till one sad morn, his daughter, full of glee,
    Came to him with a young man arm in arm,
And cheeks that blushed like pearl-white clouds caressing
    The warm, magnetic, love-charged sun above,
And said, "O father! give your god-strown blessing
    On him and me! for, father, I'm in love!"
While the young man, half earnest, half ashamed,
Knelt with her for the blessing that she claimed.

Diogenes was slightly thunderstruck;
    And, his digestion being bad that day,
He rose and howled, "Hot curses on the luck!
    This selfish world runs all the self-same way!
You said you loved me, and I did not doubt;
    Instead of which you take this homely chub,
Admit him to your heart, and turn me out:
    Oh, never mind! I'll move back to the tub!
Give me my lantern! let me go! I vow
I'll search the world for honest women, now!"

She twined her soft arms round his stubborn feet,
    She prayed him with her hands, her eyes, her lips;
Strove the dear, dreadful exigence to meet,
    And show him that 'twas not a love-eclipse;
She said, "O father, know that you are still
    All the world to me! but I have discovered
Another world: I have two hearts to fill;
    But I adore you more!" and then she hovered
Deftly between the young man and the old,
Who formed a contrast striking to behold.

"Befriend me, O my father, for I need
    Much more now your protection! I am just

"SIR, I AM YOUR DAUGHTER, IF YOU PLEASE."

First Chain.

A poor, weak girl, whose only strength, indeed,
    Is all with others—is her love and trust.
I can not live without you; this sweet man
    Has won my heart, but not away from yours;
He crowds me nearer to you; 'tis the plan
    The gods have made; 'tis why the race endures.
The passion-waves that through me surge and dart,
Sink deeper still your love into my heart.

"My love has not division, but increase;
    O father, listen to me! do not move
Your cherished face away; my life must cease,
    In this new life of love, without your love.
For my sweet mother's sake—whose heart stood still
    In its first glow of greeting for me—listen!
Your form my woman's fancy yet shall fill;
    Your dear eyes in my heart's eyes e'er shall glisten;
And all I ask, father whom I adore,
Is only just one husband, and no more!"

And here the legend stops; I can not prove
    How it turned out; but if I judge aright,
The mean old idiot trampled on her love
    With the iron shoes of jealousy and spite.
At least I learn that he was every bit
    A cynic, at near eighty, when his dim
Old soul left earth, which, though he hated it,
    He lived in longer than it wanted him.
Like some to-day, he gave this world a curse,
Because he could not have the universe.

    Grandmother SMITH (*a sweet, but hard-headed old lady*).
A mean old selfish, undeserving brute.
    Old Mr. READING (EDITH's *father*).
'Tis very strange that any man should step
With his own selfish fancy, pride, or spleen,
Betwixt his daughter and her happiness.
    SCHOOL-MASTER (*aside*), *glancing at Mr.* READING *and* EDITH.
Curious, indeed. These legends will not hit

The targets they are aimed at. Oh, the coats—
The neatly fitted coats, that hang upon
The hall-racks of man's nature, waiting long—
Waiting in vain—for him to put them on!
 [*Aloud*]
Now, with renewed attention, let us hear
Another of old Farmer Stebbins' wails,
Uttered last summer, when that modern craze,
Base-ball, was driving all the nation wild.
 Harry (*the tall young man*).
Base-ball!—the king of all our manly sports!
 Isabel (*the black-eyed girl*).
Base-ball! another man-made tournament,
Where woman views the skill and strength of man.
 Squire Stout.
Base-ball!—a mighty killin' waste o' time.
 Grandmother Smith (*the sweet, but hard-headed old lady*).
Base-ball! the bosom-friend of heart-disease
And enemy of whole and shapely hands.
 Harry (*hastily concealing a damaged knuckle*).
Who reads the Stebbins letter?
 School-master.
       David, here.
 David (*the short, fat young man*).

FARMER STEBBINS AT THE BAT.

Dear Brother John: Brooklyn, *July* 5.
We got here safe, my good old wife an' me,
An' then I strolled out to the Park, to see what I could see.
Some fellows there was playin' ball—an' with a waggish smile
One chap inquired of me if I wouldn't like to play a while;
For I'd made some remarks about the way the game was run,
An' maybe I'd take hold, he said, an' show 'em how 'twas done.

I used to play, some years ago, when youth still lingered near,
Before three hundred pounds of flesh impaired my runnin' gear;
An' so I said, "All right, I'm in; I'll give the ball a whack,
For I don't like to have old age invite me to stan' back;"

First Chain.

An' so I spoke up to'm an' said, with quite a limber tongue,
"I'll show you how we used to play when your old dads was young."

"Of course you'll stan' up to the rules?" the waggish chap inquired;
"An' will you pitch or catch?" Says I, "I'll catch, if so desired."
An' then they brought a muzzle out an' strapped it to my head,
To keep my mug from gettin' scraped by some one's bat, they said.
But I didn't mind; I says, "All right; just trim me up complete,
Providin' you don't tie no wires aroun' my hands nor feet."

But when I caught their pesky ball, I yelled out with a groan,
"Good sakes alive! I didn't suppose you played it with a stone!"
Then they all laughed, and says, "Of course this ain't no two old cat!"
An' laughed again, when I remarked, "I'm sensible of that;
But when *we* used to play base-ball we wouldn't have thought 'twas smart
To pelt each other with a chunk of old man Pharaoh's heart!"

Then they all laughed again, an' said I'd better take the field;
An' I remarked, "I'm used to that" (a fact quite unconcealed);
An' so I toddled off, an' stood, without a word to say,
Until "a hot ball," as they said, came purrin' down my way;
It landed somewhere on my frame, uncommon hard an' square,
An' I laid down, reached up my han's, an' wildly clasped it there.

An' then they laughed an' cheered, an' said I'd "caught it on the fly."
"I caught it on my stomach, if I'm any judge," says I.
An' then they laughed an' cheered some more, an' said, "Our side is in,
An' it is our turn at the bat, an' your turn to begin."
An' then I grasped the ball-club tight, an' says unto them all,
"I'll show you how to treat a hard an' unregenerate ball."

The fellow that propelled the thing wouldn't throw it square an' straight;
He'd make a sort of cow-like kick, an' pitch it like a quait;
So when I struck, with my whole firm of muscle, brain, an' heart,
The fierce blow found the ball an' club some several rods apart;
An' leanin' up, an' strikin' 'gainst the atmosphere instead,
Produced an unforeseen result, an' laid me on my head.

"One strike!" the fellow that they call the "emperor" loudly cried.
"It's full as much as that," I says, a-perchin' on my side.
"Play ball!" he shouted. An' I says, "It ain't so much like play
As some things I have seen; but then no matter; fire away!"
An' so he fired; whereat the ball benumbed each finger's-end,
Then cuffed my sufferin' ears, like some enraged maternal friend.

"Foul!" shouted loud the emperor, then, in accents loud an' high.
"You're right again; it's foul indeed, an' painful too," says I;
An' then I thought, "I'll wipe that ball half-way out of existence,
Or lay right down here an' expire, with mourners at a distance."
An' straightenin' back, I gave the thing a self-benumbin' blow,
An' sent it wobblin' through the air; an' then they shouted, "Go!"

Now I was kind of turned around 'bout where I did belong,
An' nimble as an elephant, I struck my bearin's wrong;
I stood the emperor on his head, I run the catcher down,
I barked my waggish friend's left shin, before he turned me roun';
An' then he yelled, "Pick up your heels!" an' fool-bewildered quite,
I stopped an' looked, an' said, "They're here! I've got 'em on all right!"

An' then they laughed an' cheered some more, an' said, "Go! make your base!"
An' off I went, with quickened breath, an' heat-illumined face;
I give no heed unto the world; but, thunderin' straight ahead,
Produced an earthquake in that Park by my resistless tread;
An' then I stubbed my off big toe, an' hadn't time to rise,
An' rolled three quarters of the way, to my base, and surprise.

"Out on a fly!" the emperor says, a-brushin' off his sleeve.
"Out on a bender, I should think," I says, prepared to leave;
"This game has too much earnestness to make it play for me;
It's full of hardship for to do, however nice to see.
The easiest way to play base-ball, is to sit back an' tell
How things we never could have done could be done twice as well."

Then Sister Is'bel Sunnyhopes, to my intense surprise,
Drove up an' took me in, with tears an' laughter in her eyes:

"PRODUCED AN UNFORESEEN RESULT."

"Miss Isabel," I humbly said, "it always seems to me,
The bigger fool I make myself, the more you're there to see.
I'll furnish you with candy all the rest your nat'ral life
If you won't pick this picnic up, an' take it to my wife."

SCHOOL-MASTER.
I trust henceforth our good but green old friend
May stay where balls will miss him. But one tale
Reminds us of another (although how,
I can not quite explain; we do not see
All of the gold or leaden links that bind
Our many thoughts together).
                          I will read
A legend of old Sicily's Syracuse.
    Reads:

DIONYSIUS'S MIRROR.

Old King Dionysius, insanely ambitious,
  Who stabled his prisoners *en masse*,
And (their sufferings to hear) built a great prison-ear,
  Thus embalming himself as an ass;
Contentless with hearing the words which, unfearing,
  His sufferers treated him to,
And which, unrestrained, very likely contained
  More truth than he cared to pull through;

Called up a magician, of high-born position,
  And said, with a cold, cruel grin,
"Now make me a mirror, much stronger and clearer
  Than any that ever has been.
Of methods make use, that will quick reproduce
  Every scene that its surface may hold;
The forms and the features of all of these creatures
  And all they have done, shall be told."

This high-born magician, with skilful ambition
  (The world was alive in those days,
And "magic" is science concealed in appliance),
  Proceeded the mirror to raise.

'Twas silver well burnished; and silently furnished
    The pictures that came to its eyes;
And the place in a minute, to those who were in it,
    Seemed wondrously doubled in size.

Its woes, too, were doubled; and they who were troubled
    With sickness and hunger and pain,
Felt needlessly shocked, and their sufferings mocked
    By a levity brutal and vain.
Such infamous "mercies," they thanked with their curses;
    Such "luxuries" wakened their ire;
Of the gods they implored that the king might be stored
    In a mirror-walled prison of fire.

Slow or fleetly, at last, but a year had gone past,
    When a general order there came,
That this wonderful mirror—this optical sneerer—
    Be moved from its rock-girded frame.
The tablet of malice was borne to the palace,
    And met by the tyrant's best sneer,
Who said to his court, "We will see, for our sport,
    What the rascals have done for a year."

Then the noted magician, with skill and precision
    (For science was known in those days,
And arts have been lost, as we know to our cost),
    Uncovered the view to their gaze.
But a sight of such woe as may few ever know,
    Came forth on the silvery sheen;
Such terror-strewn languor, such pain-sharpened anger,
    Had ne'er in a palace been seen!

No look of despair but displayed itself there;
    No sorrow but stepped out to view;
No terrible death but here drew its last breath;
    No horror was ever more true.
But each pain-harrowed face bent its look to one place;
    All curses one way seemed to turn;
And the guests, past surprise, raised their horrified eyes,
    The cause of such hate to discern.

Not yet.—'Twas not seen. But the silvery sheen
    Showed pictures more terribly new;
Black serpents untwined from the heart and the mind
    Of the wretches that crowded in view;
Black serpents of hate crept like creatures of fate
    With tongues that were forkèd and red;
All crept to one place; and the guests sought to trace
    Where 'twas that the reptiles had fled.

Not yet.—'Twas not seen. But there came, sharp and keen,
    From above, blinding lightnings of wrath;
They swept down below, as to see the dread woe,
    Then flashed on the same upward path.
"May the gods turn the luck of whomever that struck!"
    Said the guests, nearly frenzied with fear,
As they gazed, full of dread, at the mystery o'erhead,
    To witness the victim appear.

Not yet.—From beneath—living blades of the sheath
    Of Hades, thick padded with flame—
Rose devils of fire, half in sport, half in ire,
    And scowled at some object of shame.
They motioned to him, with ape-grimaces grim,
    And meaningly pointed below,
As to say, "'Twill not be very long, ere you see
    What our grim hospitalities show."

"Raise the screen! raise the screen, and display the whole scene!"
    Said the tyrant, with half-trembling glee:
"Let us view that unknown, with such hot curses strown;
    Worst prisoner of all he must be!"
The magician, fear-pale, slowly drew back the veil,
    And there, 'mid his palace's pelf,
With his ear to The Ear, and his face white with fear,
    Was old Dionysius himself!

"Break the sorcerous liar! Melt it up with white fire!"
    Yelled the tyrant, in frenzied dismay:
It was done; but still there, on the walls of the air,
    Came the picture, by night and by day.

And no doubt when he stood 'mid the bad and the good,
    His lot for the future to draw,
  In the record of shame that was marked with his name,
    That scene of the mirror he saw.

  Squire STOUT.
By George! that never happened in this world.
  Grandmother SMITH.
I think it is a sort of parable.
  SCHOOL-MASTER.
Our deeds—our thoughts—our feelings—all are cast
In mirror-pictures, that shall never fade.
Oft by Fate's touch—oft'ner by our own acts—
The veil will rise, and show us what we are—
What we have been—what we through self must be.
And oft in pictures where we think to view
Others well sketched, is our own image seen!
  Squire STOUT (*aside*).
We do not pay the teacher, I'll be bound,
To loaf about, and spout such stuff as this.
  Grandmother SMITH.
Forgive me, if I think the legends told
Thus far, have been somewhat unanimous
Against old men—whom, as a rule, I like
(Perhaps because I liked them while still young).
But will you hear a legend now, of one
Who lived within the suburbs of a small
Old inland city that I used to know,
And who, I think, will preach that some old men
Are kindly, generous, true, and sensible?
  Reads:

UNCLE NATE'S FUNERAL.

'Twas not at all like those you see of ordinary men;
'Twas such as never could occur, excepting now and then.
For Uncle Nate had studied hard upon it, night and day,
And planned it all—while yet alive—in his peculiar way.
"I've managed other men's remains," he said, in quiet tone.
"And now I'll make a first-class try to regulate my own."

"AND THEY HAVE SCAMPERED FAR AND NEAR, AND PICKED THE FRESHEST FLOWERS."

First Chain.

And so, a month before his death, he wrote the details down,
For friends to print, when he was dead, and mail throughout the town.

The paper said: "I've figured close, and done the best I knew,
To have a good large funeral, when this shortish life was through;
I've thought about it night and day, I've brooded o'er the same,
Until it almost seemed a task to wait until it came.
Especially as my good wife has wandered on ahead,
And all the children we possessed have many years been dead;
And now I'll tell you what I want my friends and foes to do—
I'm sorry that I can't be here to push the matter through:

"I do not want to hire a hearse, with crape around it thrown:
I'm social like, and am not used to riding round alone.
Bring my old wagon, into which the children used to climb,
Until I've taken on a drive full twenty at a time:
We've loafed along the country roads for many pleasant hours,
And they have scampered far and near, and picked the freshest flowers:
And I would like to have them come, upon my burial day,
And ride with me, and talk to me, and sing along the way.

"I want my friend the minister—the best of preacher-folks,
With whom I've argued, prayed, and wept, and swapped a thousand jokes—
To *talk* a sermon to the friends, and make it sweet, but strong;
And recollect, I don't believe in speeches over-long.
And tell him, notwithstanding all his eloquence and worth,
'Twon't be the first time I have slept when he was holding forth.
I'd like two texts; and one shall be by Bible covers pressed,
And one from outside, that shall read, 'He did his level best.'

"And any one I've given help—to comfort or to save—
Just bring a flower, or sprig of green, and throw it in the grave.
Please have a pleasant, social time round the subscriber's bier,
And no one but my enemies must shed a single tear.
You simply say, 'Old Uncle Nate, whatever may befall,
Is having probably to-day the best time of us all!

He's shaking hands, two at a clip, with several hundred friends,
And giving us who stay behind good gilt-edged recommends!'"

They tried to follow all the rules that Uncle Nate laid down:
When he was dead they came to him from every house in town.
The children did their best to sing, but could not quite be heard;
The parson had a sermon there, but did not speak a word.
Of course they buried him in flowers, and kissed him as he lay,
For not a soul in all that town but he had helped some way;
But when they tried to mould his mound without the tear-drop's
    leaven,
There rose loud sobs that Uncle Nate could almost hear in heaven.

                    [*Clock strikes twelve. All rise, and disperse in
                           silence, for they all knew Uncle Nate.*

SECOND CHAIN.

Second Chain.

SCENE, *the front parlor of a city residence. It is prettily and daintily furnished. Bows of ribbon adorn almost everything, except a young gentleman, who has called. Conspicuous among the pictures on the walls are those of a nice old lady and gentleman, who look as if they might be the grandfather and grandmother of some young lady. Enter a young lady, seats herself at friendly but respectful distance from the young gentleman, and gazes at him doubtingly.*

ETHEL (*the young lady*).
You say you love me; but how do I know
   That all of the scattered words you send,
Bring truth with them? the tongue may glow
   With thoughts that leap from a friend to a friend,
Or fly with Fancy's mottled wing;
But Love, dear friend, is a sacred thing.
Love is not tinsel, silver, or gold:
   It is a fragment of Heaven's own gate,
   Broken in halves by God's hand, Fate,
And given two kindred spirits bold,
   Who would colonize in our Earth unknown:
'Tis whispered them, "You may be thrown
Far apart; be passion-whirled
To different sides of that dizzy world;
But search for each other, far and near,
With a painful hope, and a joyful fear.
Search, through fair or stormy weather,
   Until the halves of this broken gem
Cling and clasp and weld together,
   With the power that attracted them.
Then shall be bartered Love's true token;
Then shall The Heart's Password be spoken."

Dearest of comrades, how can I know
  That yours is the soul that is seeking mine,
Until the gems to each other glow—
  Until you speak the words divine?

> [*The portrait of the young lady's grandmother upon the wall seems to smile approvingly at this speech; that of her grandfather has a somewhat puzzled look.*

FITZ CLINTONNE (*the young man, bashfully, and somewhat awkwardly*).
Yes, you are right: my tongue *is* dull—
  Words step slowly, and far apart;
Fogs float my small intellect full—
  Creeping between the head and heart.
Something thrusts from me, ever yet,
  Things that I do not want to say;
Something makes my tongue forget
  Gems I remember, when away.
Several times I have had The Speech
  Close to my blind tongue's groping reach;
Several times, my foremost word
  Stumbled against some small event,
Mean, and pitiful, and absurd,
  As if by a mischief-bureau sent.

> [*The portrait of the young lady's grandmother on the wall seems to smile approvingly, with a half-triumphant expression; that of the grandfather appears to put on a sympathizing look.*

FITZ CLINTONNE (*continuing*).
That time in the shady, flower-breathed grove,
  Your hand on my arm, we slowly walked,
My tongue of a sudden fell in love—
  Cupid himself!—how I could have talked!
But ere the oration was half begun,
  A cow broke through the confounded fences—
Charged on us, with a swinging run—
  ETHEL.
Scared me half-way out of my senses—

Second Chain.

FITZ CLINTONNE.
And so the words my soul would say,
Were drowned in a loud inglorious " Whey!"
My word-supply-car jumped the track,
In shunting that wretched milk-train back.
One time we floated the marching lake
    They call a river—the key was mine!
The billows of speech began to break—
    They soon would have brought The Word divine!
But an envious fish crept round our way—
The only one that we caught that day—
And nabbed your hook—and my oration—
    Ere it was half begun—was o'er.
    ETHEL (*animatedly*).
One of the beauties of creation!
    Weighed ten pounds and a half, or more!
    FITZ CLINTONNE.
The fish, I suppose you mean. One eve,
Just as the twilight prepared to leave,
We sat and looked at a silver paring
    Called the new moon—near a diamond-star
Which the sweet blue-eyed sky was wearing—
    Words rushed straight to me, from afar;
Stopped at my heart, then sought the tongue;
Never such words were said or sung!
But o'er our veranda, just in time
To wed the ridiculous and sublime,
Crept a small mouse—bright-eyed and fleet—
    ETHEL.
And I screamed like a panthress, and jumped six feet!

    [*The face of the grandfather on the wall actually seems to grin; that of the grandmother lengthens in pictorial sympathetic fright, and her arms appear to stretch suddenly towards the lower folds of her dress.*

    FITZ CLINTONNE (*aside*).
If I would not be left out of sight,
    An answer to-day I *must* insist on;

For Fitz Cumlippitt is coming, to-night,
   And he has a tongue like an engine-piston.
He will say so many soft words to 'er,
The Password will be amongst them, sure;
At least, she will think it is— O shade
Of every talker that e'er was made,
Of gossips, and lawyers, and auctioneers,
Of orators, poets, and talking seers,
Lend me your tongues—or my murderers be;
For I shall die, if she doesn't wed me!
   [*Aloud*]
Ethel, I love you. Let it suffice
My words are earnest, if not o'er-nice.
'Mid all this century's arts and shams,
My love is as firm as
   HUCKSTER (*in the street*).
               Soft shell c-l-a-m-s!
   FITZ CLINTONNE (*recovering*).
Fie on the villain! Ethel, my heart
Is yours forever; we must not part.
Often my soul, in some lonely spot,
Reaches for yours, and finds it not;
And breaks into still, tumultuous sobs—
Longing—longing—for—
   HUCKSTER (*in the street*).
               Crabs an' l-o-b-s—
L-o-b-s-t-e-r-s!
   FITZ CLINTONNE (*indignantly*).
            Fie on the sordid wretch,
Collapsing my speech, with his mouth astretch!
Ethel, I need, for my heart's repose—
   VOICE (*in the street*).
Cash fur ol' clo's—ol' clo-'s ol' c-l-o-o-s—
   FITZ CLINTONNE (*tenderly*).
If you will be my life-heart-friend,
You shall have always
   VOICE (*in the street*).
               B-o-i-l-e-r-s to mend!

FITZ CLINTONNE (*resolutely*).
You shall have always love and rest,
  Soothing you through life's varied scenes;
Safe in our Boston bright home-nest,
  We will e'er live on
    Female HUCKSTER (*in street, shrilly, and in a tone of interrogation*).
              Pork an' b-e-a-n-s?
  FITZ CLINTONNE (*despairingly*).
Ever 'tis thus. You see I may
  As well talk Greek, or Zulu, or Hindoo;
Chaos intrudes, whatever I say;
  I will close my speech.
    ETHEL (*smiling*).
                    Or perhaps, the window.
  FITZ CLINTONNE (*after obeying with alacrity*).
Ethel, I love you. My love is pure
And fresh from the soul, and must endure.
Its fountains shall never cease to flow!
  ETHEL (*positively*).
Oh, but men's love is *never* so!
  FITZ CLINTONNE (*solemnly*).
Ethel, have you one case in view,
Where man to woman has proved untrue?
  ETHEL (*readily*).
Thousands and thousands and thousands! no man
Has walked the world since the world began,
As true to the woman who loved him truly,
As she to him.
  FITZ CLINTONNE.
              You speak unduly.
But list while I tell you, second-hand,
What a young man in Austria-land
Stood for the girl he loved. 'Tis fit
To say that he stood, as you'll admit.

> [*Draws a magazine from his pocket, and prepares to read. The young lady arranges a series of furtive yawns; the faces on the wall assume a look of stoical endurance.*

FITZ CLINTONNE *reads:*

THE HERO OF THE TOWER.

Long time ago, when Austria was young,
There came a herald to Vienna's gates,
Bidding the city fling them open wide
Upon a certain day; for then the king
Would enter, with his shining retinue.

Forthwith the busy streets were pleasure paths;
And that which seemed but now a field of toil,
With weeds of turbulence and tricky greed,
Flashed into gardens blooming full of flowers.
Beauty blushed deeper, now the rising sun
Of royalty upon it was to shine;
Wealth cast its nets of tinsel and of gold
To catch the kingly eye; and wisdom merged
Itself into the terms of an address,
Which the old mayor sat up nights to learn.
No maiden fluttered through the narrow streets
That pondered not what ribbons she should wear;
No window on the long procession's route
But had its tenants long engaged ahead.

But the old sexton of St. Joseph's Church
Moped dull and sulky through the smiling crowd,
A blot upon the city's pleasure-page.
"What runs wrong with you, uncle?" was the cry;
"You, who have been the very youngest boy
Of all the old men that the city had;
Who loved processions more than perquisites,
And rolled a gala-day beneath your tongue:
What rheumatism has turned that temper lame?
Speak up, and make your inward burden ours."

The old man slowly walked until he came
Unto the market-place; then feebly stopped,
As if to talk; and a crowd gathered soon,

Second Chain.

As men will, when a man has things to say.
And thus he spoke: "For fifty years and more,
I have been sexton of St. Joseph's Church;
St. Joseph's would have fared ill but for me.
And though my friend the priest may smile at this,
And wink at you an unbelieving eye,
My office shines in heaven as well as his.
Although it was not mine to make the church
Godly, I kept it clean; and that stands next.
If I have broke one circle of my sphere,
Let some one with straight finger trace it out.

"And no procession, in these fifty years,
Has marched the streets with aught like kingly tread,
But on the summit of St. Joseph's spire
I stood erect and waved a welcome-flag,
With scanty resting-place beneath my feet,
And the wild breezes clutching at my beard.
It took some nerve to stand so near to heaven
And fling abroad its colors. Try it, priest.

"But I am old; most of my manhood's fire
Is choked in cold white ashes; and my nerves
Tremble in every zephyr like the leaves.
What can I do?—the flag must not be missed
From the cathedral's summit! I've no son,
Or he should bear the banner, or my curse.
I have a daughter; she shall wave the flag!

"And this is how my child shall wave the flag:
Ten suitors has she; and the valiant one
Who, strong of heart and will, can climb that perch,
And do what I so many times have done,
Shall take her hand from mine at his descent.
Speak up, Vienna lads! and recollect
How much of loveliness faint heart e'er won."

Then there was clamor in the callow breasts
Of the Vienna youth; for she was far

The sweetest blossom of that city's vines.
Many a youngster's eye climbed furtively
Where the frail spire-tip trembled in the breeze,
Then wandered to the cot wherein she dwelt;
But none spoke up, till Gabriel Petersheim,
Whose ear this proclamation strange had reached,
Came rushing through the crowd, and boldly said:

"I am your daughter's suitor, and the one
She truly loves; but scarce can gain a smile
Until I win her father's heart as well;
And you, old man, have frowned on me, and said
I was too young, too frivolous, too wild,
And had not manhood worthy of her hand.
Mark me to-morrow as I mount yon spire,
And mention, when I bring the flag to you,
Whether 'twas ever waved more gloriously."

And thus the old man answered: "Climb your way;
And if a senseful breeze should push you off,
And break that raw and somewhat worthless neck,
I could not greatly mourn; but climb your way,
And you shall have the girl if you succeed."

High on the giddy pinnacle, next day
Waited the youth; but not till evening's sun
Marched from the western gates, that tardy king
Rode past the church. And though young Gabriel's nerves
Were weakened by fatigue and want of food,
He pleased the people's and the monarch's eye,
And flashed a deeper thrill of love through one
Who turned her sweet face often up to him,
And whose true heart stood with him on the tower.

Now, when the kingly pageant all had passed,
He folded up the flag, and with proud smiles
And prouder heart prepared him to descend.
But the small trap-door through which he had crept,
Had by some rival's hand been barred! and he,

Second Chain.

With but a hand-breadth's space where he might cling,
Was left alone, to live there, or to die.

Guessing the truth, or shadow of the truth,
He smiled, at first, and said: "Well, let them voice
Their jealousy by such a paltry trick!
They laugh an hour; my laugh will longer be!
Their joke will soon be dead, and I released."
But an hour, and two others, slowly came,
And then he murmured, "This is no boy's sport;
It is a silent signal, which means 'Death!'"

He shouted, but no answer came to him;
Not even an echo, on that lofty perch.
He waved his hands in mute entreaty; but
The darkness crept between him and his friends.

A half-hour seemed an age, and still he clung.
He looked down at the myriad city lights,
Twinkling like stars upon a lowlier sky,
And prayed: "O blessèd city of my birth!
In which full many I love, and one o'er-well,
Or I should not be feebly clinging here,
Is there not 'mongst those thousands one kind heart
To help me? or must I come back to you
Crashing my way through grim, untimely death?"
Rich sounds of mirth came faintly—but no help.

Another hour went by, and still he clung.
He braced himself against the rising breeze,
And wrapped the flag around his shivering form,
And thus he prayed unto the merry winds:

"O breeze! you bear no tales of truer love
Than I can give you at this lonely height!
Tell but my danger to the heart I serve,
And she will never rest till I am free!"
The winds pressed hard against him as he clung,
And well nigh wrenched him from that scanty hold,
But made no answer to his piteous plea.

Hour after hour went by, and still he held—
Weak, dizzy, reeling—to his narrow perch.
It was a clear and queenly summer night;
And every star seemed hanging from the sky,
As if 'twere bending down to look at him.
And thus he prayed to the far-shining stars:

"O million worlds, peopled perhaps like this,
Can you not see me, clinging helpless here?
Can you not flash a message to some eye,
Or throw your influence on some friendly brain
To rescue me?"—A million sweet-eyed stars
Gave smiles to the beseecher, but no help.

And so the long procession of the night
Marched slowly by, and each scarce hour was hailed
By the great clock beneath; and still he clung
Unto the frail preserver of his life,
And held, not for his life, but for his love.—
Held while the spiteful breezes wrenched at him;
Held while the chills of midnight crept through him;
While Hope and Fear made him their battle-ground,
And ravaged fiercely through his heart and brain.
He moaned, he wept, he prayed again; he prayed—
Grown desperate and half raving in his woe—
To everything in earth, or air, or sky:
To the fair streets, now still and silent grown;
To the cold roofs, now stretched 'twixt him and aid;
To the dumb, distant hills that heedless slept;
To the white clouds that slowly fluttered past;
To his lost mother in the sky above;
And then he prayed to God.

      About that time,
The maiden, who, half anxious and half piqued
That her through all the evening he'd not sought,
Had sunk into a restless, thorn-strown sleep,
Dreamed that she saw her lover on the tower,
Clinging for life; and with a scream uprose,

Second Chain.

And rushed to the old sexton's yielding door,
Granting no peace to him until he ran
To find the truth, and give the boy release.

An hour ere sunrise he crept feebly down,
Grasping the flag, and claiming his fair prize.
But what a wreck to win a blooming girl!
His cheeks were wrinkled, and of yellow hue;
His eyes were sunken; and his curling hair
Gleamed white as snow upon the distant Alps.

But the young maiden clasped his weary head
In her white arms, and soothed him like a child;
And said, "You lived a life of woe for me
Up on the spire, and now look old enough
Even to please my father; but soon I
Will nurse you back into your youth again."

And soon the tower bells sung his wedding song.
The old-young man was happy; and they both,
Cheered by the well-earned bounty of the king,
Lived many years within Vienna's gates.

[*A brief interval of silence follows. The portraits of the old people on the wall seem to have awakened; their forms have the appearance of stretching, after a nice little nap.* ETHEL *looks dreamily out of the window, yawns in her eyes, at a flirtation going on across the street.*

FITZ CLINTONNE.
Was he not faithful!—answer me!
ETHEL.
Yes, I confess; 'tis only fair
To admit that a man will faithful be
  If placed on a tower and locked up there.
    FITZ CLINTONNE (*thoughtfully, and aside*).
A turn of the story I didn't foresee.
[*Aloud*] Ethel, I love you!—I am the youth
Upon that tower; and I wave, in truth,

The banner of love; for all can see,
Who have much knowledge of you and me,
My unhid passion!—but far from reach
You are locked away by my lack of speech.
The walls of my reticence gloom about;—
Ethel, for Heaven's sake, let me out!
I WILL break through, with Love's strong arts,
And give you the password of our hearts!
The words are coming!

    [*An empty express wagon rushes like a peal of thunder along the street, shaking the house to its very foundations, and overwhelming all other sound.* FITZ CLINTONNE *sinks back in hopeless silence.* ETHEL *laughs drearily. The portraits on the wall vibrate, and a sealed envelope drops from the grandmother's picture—almost as it might be from the venerable lady's pocket. Her face looks as if she were glad to get rid of it.* ETHEL *picks it up.*]

ETHEL.
Another poem, I do declare!—
  From a cousin I will not name;
  Placed (the poem) within the frame,
Just to help keep the canvas there.
A maiden lady of—certain age,
Thrilled with a mild poetic rage;
She sends us copies of every rhyme;
We do not open them, half the time. [*Breaks the envelope.*]
But this I will read. And you may know
By the title, why I do so.
  Reads:

A WOMAN'S DEVOTION; OR, TRUE TO BROTHER SPEAR.

    I can't decide why Brother Spear
      Was never joined to me;
    It wasn't because the good old dear
      Hadn't every chance to be!

Second Chain.

If Poetry remarked, one time,
    That "Womanhood is true,"
It's more than probable that I'm
    The one it had in view;
For search the city, low and high,
    Inquire, both far and near—
There's none will say but what that I
    Was true to Brother Spear!

I mothered all his daughters when
    Their mamma's life cut short,
Although they didn't—now or then—
    So much as thank me for't;
I laughed down my interior rage,
    And said I didn't care,
When his young son, of spank'ble age,
    Reduced my surplus hair;
I called and called and called there; why
    He was not in, seemed queer;
The neighbors, even, owned that I
    Was true to Brother Spear!

I hired a sitting in the church,
  Near him, but corner-wise,
So his emotions I could search,
  With my devoted eyes;
And when the sermon used to play
  On love, divine and free,
I nodded him, as if to say,
  "It's hitting you and me!"
He went and took another pew—
  Of "thousand tongues" in fear;
I also changed, and still was true
  To good old Brother Spear!

Poor man!—I recollect he spoke,
  One large prayer-meeting night,
And told how little we must look,
  In Heaven's majestic sight;
He said, Unworthy he had been,
  By Conscience e'er abhorred,
To be a door-keeper within
  The temple of The Lord;
And that his place forevermore,
  Undoubtedly and clear,
Was mainly back *behind* the door—
  Poor humble Brother
    Spear!

And then *I* rose and made a speech,
  Brimful of soul distress;
And told them how words could not reach
  My own unworthiness;
Though orphanage I tried to soothe,
  And helpless widowerhood,
To tell the incandescent truth,
  I too felt far from good;

Second Chain.

And that a trembling heart and mind
    Compelled it to appear
That my place also was behind
    The door, with Brother Spear!

Poor man! he ne'er was heard, they say,
    Again to gladly speak;
He took down sick the following day,
    And died within a week.
One prayer they often heard him give:
    That, if his days were o'er,
I still upon the earth might live,
    A hundred years or more.
As his betrothed I figure, now,
    And drop the frequent tear;
And his relations all will vow
    I'm true to Brother Spear!

[*The portraits on the wall look quite interested and considerably amused.* ETHEL *tears the paper into fragments.*

ETHEL (*pouting*).
  Senseless creature! If I had known
    What 'twas she wrote, I'd have not begun it!
    FITZ CLINTONNE (*laughing*).
  But she was faithful, I will own;
    Love so fervent—how could he shun it?
    ETHEL.
  He couldn't, except through Death's design.
    FITZ CLINTONNE.
  No more, dear Ethel, than you can mine.
  Perhaps, somewhere, she may woo and win
    This scornful man, if she works and waits:
  For passion is oft concealed within
    A cloak that its object loathes and hates.
  And true devotion and love, they say,
  ("It's dogged as does it") will win, some day.
  Still, one must walk a hard road yet,
    To always pursue, and ne'er be met;
  But man is equal to that same task.
  Hear of another faithful one— [*Draws a newspaper.*
    ETHEL (*in mild consternation*).
  Oh, it is more than I could ask!
    FITZ CLINTONNE (*resolutely*).
  No, don't mention it!
    ETHEL.
              Then don't you!
    FITZ CLINTONNE (*resolutely*).
  Judge if I may not, when 'tis done;
    Yes, you must hear it, without fail!
  A man who waited his whole life through:
    Hear the poor fellow's doleful tale.
    Reads:

TWELVE O'CLOCK: A LEGEND OF BROOKLYN.

  "'Do I love you?' Oh, but listen!"—
  And he saw her dark eyes glisten,
    With a gentle joy that filled him—
    With a passion-wave that thrilled him:

Second Chain.

"'Do I love you?' ask the ages
Front of this life's blotted pages—
Cycles that our minds forget,
But our souls remember yet—
If the strands they saw us twine
In great moments half divine,
Can not stand against the cold
Voice and touch of senseless gold?
How can Wealth forbid the meeting
Of two hearts that blend in beating?
How can Thrift presume to fashion
Heaven's eternal love and passion?
Listen!—if 'tis not o'er-soon,
Come to-morrow-day at noon;—
On that glad—that mournful day
When my girlhood creeps away—
On that day—the understood
Birthday of my womanhood—
Come! and, joined in hand as heart,
We will walk no more apart.
Meet me—do not let me wait—
By this iron—this golden gate—
When, its mid-day hour to tell,
Rings the silvery court-house bell.

"Should I fail you, dear, to-morrow,
Go away, but not in sorrow;
There be many ways may meet
Fetters round a maiden's feet.
There be watchers—there be spies—
There be jealous tongues and eyes;
Many hate my love for you,
And would cut our life in two.
Oh, they guard me all the time,
As if loving were a crime!

"Should I fail the second morrow,
Hope from next day you must borrow;
If I fail you then—endure;
Hope and trust be still the cure.

Naught on earth has power—has art
Long to hold us two apart;
None but God were equal to it,
And I know He would not do it.
I will come to you, indeed;
You would wait, love, were there need?"
And he said, with brave endeavor,
"I will wait for you forever.
Each day I shall come to you,
Till you come, and find me true.
Each day hear the hopeful swell
Of the mid-day court-house bell."

So, next day, he stood and waited
For the soul his soul had mated;
Saw the clock's black finger climb
To its topmost round of time—
Heard the mighty metal throat
Sing afar its mid-day note;
Listened, with a nervous thrill,
And his warm heart standing still,
Glanced about, with keen desire,
And his yearning soul afire;
Searched, and searched, with jealous care—
Searched—but saw no loved one there.
"'Should I fail you, dear, to-morrow,
Go away, but not in sorrow;'
'Twas her word," he softly said:
"Be she living, be she dead,
Still my heart is scant of fear;
She will some time meet me here.
My sad soul I will employ
With to-morrow's destined joy;
Here is happiness for me,
Living o'er what is to be.
She will come—her love to tell—
With to-morrow's mid-day bell."

So, next day, he watched and waited,
With a heart by hope elated;

Second Chain.

Peering—searching for a face
Full of love-exalted grace.
But his glance crept far and wide
With some fear it could not hide;
Crept across the grimy pavement,
Moaning in its dull enslavement;
Roamed the long streets, empty-seeming,
Though with lovely faces gleaming;
Shivered, as with landscape drear,
'Neath a blue sky, bright and clear;
For the bell, with sorrowing strain,
Called her to his side in vain.
"'If I fail the second morrow,
Hope from next day you must borrow:'
'Twas her word," he bravely said:
"Let to-morrow stand instead."
Still upon his heart there fell
Shadows from the mid-day bell.

Day by day he watched and waited,
By cold Disappointment fated;
Bit by bit his hoping ceased;
Hour by hour his faith increased.
Oft he strove to find her, then,
In her guardian's palace-den;
But the looks he met were bleak,
And the marble would not speak.
Would not show the poisoned thong
Of a dark and fiendish wrong;
Would not tell the woe and rage
Of a dreary mad-house cage,
Where the girl was kept by stealth,
Lest she claim her paltry wealth.
Could not hear her frantic prayer
That God's hand might reach her there;
Could not see her droop away
Hour by hour and day by day;
Could not feel her breath grow still
With the healing arts that kill;

Could not trace the greed that gave
Her a half-named marble grave.
Still he watched and waited well,
'Neath the weary noontide bell.

Days and weeks and months and years
Coursed the face of time, like tears;
Spring's sweet-scented mid-day air—
Summer's fierce meridian glare,
Autumn's mingled lead and gold,
Winter's murder-thrusts of cold.
Patiently he braved each one
At its mid-day cloud or sun;
Silently he turned—was gone—
Sad, desponding, and alone.
Still his famished eyes crept round,
Still he thrilled at every sound:
"'Naught on earth has power—has art
Long to hold us two apart;
None but God were equal to it,
And I know He would not do it.'
'Twas her word," he grimly said:
"She will come, alive or dead."
Pavement travellers passed him by,
Day by day, with curious eye;
Dreamers sought romance to trace
In his bronzed and fading face;
Questioners, though kind, were yet
With cold, patient silence met;
Still he watched and waited well,
By the lonely court-house bell.

Yet he came—yet crept away;
And his dark brown hair grew gray—
And his manhood's power grew spent,
And his form was thin and bent.
Poorly clad, and rough to see;
Crushed by Sickness' stern decree;
For intense compassion fit,
But still grandly scorning it.

"... A FORM—OR WAS HE DREAMING?"

Second Chain.

"He is crazed," they said, aside:
"I am sane!" his heart replied.
"'I will come to you, indeed;
You would wait, love, were there need?'
'Twas her word," he faintly said:
"Hands will meet, if hearts are wed."
Sometimes to him it would seem,
Half in earnest, half in dream,
He could view her loveliness—
He could feel her fond caress.
But some passing sound or sight
Sent the vision back to night;
And a dull and mournful knell
Seemed the leaden court-house bell.

As, one day, his weakened form
Bent before a winter storm,
As he fell—Death's fear before him,
And a veil of darkness o'er him,
Soft a voice—or was it seeming?
Full a form—or was he dreaming?
Brought a rapture that repaid
All the debts that Grief had made.
"O my love!" the words came fast;
"Do you see me, then, at last?
Do you hear me—do you feel me—
Can the world no more conceal me?
'Did I meet you?' Oh, but listen!
When released from Pain's black prison,
Long through deserts and through meadows,
Long through Death's black silent shadows,
With my soul God's help entreating,
Sought I for our place of meeting.
Oh, I crushed my arms around you,
When I found you—when I found you—
Saw you sorrow's black net weaving—
Fondly suffering—bravely grieving—
Saw the truth you could not see—
Felt your loving faith in me.

How, each day, God's help entreating,
Came I to our place of meeting!
How I hailed each coming morrow!
How I strove to soothe your sorrow!
Times, the thought would come to cheer me—
'He can see me! He can hear me!'
Then the mists of earth would screen us—
Then day's darkness stepped between us.
Yet your dear soul I could see,
Suffering still its way to me.
Pain at last has cut the tether;
Death will let us live together.
Darling, throw your arms around me!
You have found me—you have found me—
Naught on earth had power or art,
Long to hold us two apart.
None but God were equal to it,
And I knew He would not do it.
Listen! Hear the echoes swell
Of our merry wedding-bell!"

[*A few moments of phenomenal silence ensue.* ETHEL *absently toys with a musical album on the table near her; she touches the spring unconsciously, and there leaps forth in small diminutive tones an affecting little love ditty, thus, as it were, furnishing to the scene an appropriate dramatic accompaniment of soft music.*

FITZ CLINTONNE (*suddenly*).
Ethel, the bonds of speech are broken!
Now or ne'er shall the word be spoken—

[*A terrific shock of earthquake interrupts him—the first known in that city for years. Furniture commences an impromptu dance. Portraits on the wall nearly knock their heads together.* ETHEL *screams, and clings resolutely and perseveringly to* Fitz Clintonne *for protection. Their lips accidentally meet in a long and half-delirious kiss— the first they have thus far placed on record. This so absorbs the young gentleman, that, although quite scientifically inclined, he forgets to study any other of the seismic effects about him. Indeed, the earthquake almost immediately subsides.*

Ethel (*slowly unclinging herself*).
Who would have thought that—thrilled with bliss—
The Password was, after all—a kiss!

[*Portraits opposite them seem to assume a "Bless you, my children," look. The usual amount of serenity resumes its sway. Street traffic recommences its clamors, but is unheard within.*

THIRD CHAIN.

Third Chain.

SCENE I., *Christmas morning in an old-fashioned country kitchen. Culinary apparatus is lying about in a semi-orderly manner. Bunches of seed-corn are braided together by the husks over the doors. A Bible and hymn-book are on the mantel. An almanac is hanging near by. The last numbers of the Deacon's own denominational journal and the local paper of a neighboring village, rest upon a table in the corner—a pair of steel-bowed spectacles lying across them. Two cats are camping cozily and contentedly before the large kitchen stove—one of them purring softly in a half slumber, the other silent in absolute sleep.*

    Deacon KINDMAN.
Trim up the parlors, good-wife, and make them extra gay;
For *I'm* to have a party, on this cold Christmas Day:
The friends that are invited will be here—do not doubt!
I'll go myself and bring them, unless they'll come without.

Oh yes! you've been a-guessing, perhaps a month or two,
About *my* Christmas party, and what I meant to do;
The first whose invitations have all been left to me:
You're not quite sure concerning the guests you're going to see

Our children?—No, not this time; they've children of their own,
Whose Christmas-trees are bending with presents newly grown;
They've got their life-vines planted, with love-flowers all about—
Just what *we* worked so hard for, when we first started out.

Our cousins?—Well, not this time; 'tisn't what the plan intends;
They're all quite earthly-prosperous, with any amount of friends;
The world is always offering success an upward hitch;
But Christmas wasn't invented entirely for the rich.

Our preacher and his family?—They're working now, like sin,
A-sorting out the slippers and other gifts sent in;
One turkey that I know of is on their kitchen-blaze;
A cheery, popular preacher has good times, nowadays!

You don't know who you've cooked for?—Well, that *is* 'most too bad;
Of course you've no cur'os'ty—no woman ever had!
But still, your hands and heart, wife, have well nigh gone to war?
A woman works much happier, when she knows who it's for?...

I'll tell you one:—a cripple that you and I both know,
Is living in a small hut, half buried in the snow—
His body bravely struggling to coax his soul to stay;
I'm going to get that cripple, and keep him here all day.

And one's a poor old woman we've never called our friend,
But whose sad life grows heavy while struggling to its end—
Without a merry Christmas for twenty winters drear!
To-day she'll have a picnic to last her all the year.

And one's an old-style preacher; brimful of heavenly truth,
Whose eloquence lost fashion, or ran off with his youth;
And younger men and prettier, with flowery words came nigh;
And so the various churches have stood the old man by.

He tried his best to please them and serve Jehovah too—
He toiled each separate Sunday to "get up something new;"
They wanted elocution, and curvey-gestured speech!
And now this grand old preacher can't get a place to preach.

But I've a strong opinion, that angels crowd up near
That man-deserted leader, his godlike thoughts to hear;—
We'll have a Bible-chapter made over good as new,
When he to-day talks Gospel, and asks the blessing too!

"And who else?"—I have sent word to all in my mind's way,
Who can't afford a dinner that's equal to The Day;
And some good prosperous friends, too, will come with smiling face,
To keep those poor from feeling that they're a separate race.

And one of them's a neighbor; who, though sincere, no doubt,
Once couldn't quite understand me—and so we two fell out;
And every Sunday morning we've passed each other's door,
And have not known each other for fifteen years or more:

I went to him last evening, and said, "Old friend, see here;
We're both tip-top good fellows: now, doesn't it strike you queer,
That we're assisting Satan to sow the grain of strife?
Come over, sure, to-morrow, and bring along your wife.

"Just come and help us, helping some poor ones draw their loads,
Who've stalled upon the side-hills of Life's uneven roads."
He looked at me in wonder—then stood a moment still—
Then grasped my hands, and whispered, "My dear old friend, I will."

I think you're with me, good-wife, from what your features say;
And that's the kind of comp'ny we're going to have to-day—
Through which I hope a true love for all mankind may roam;
A sort of Christmas party where Christ would feel at home.

SCENE II., *a large number assembled in the parlor. It is not exactly a homogeneous company, but seems to be quite a happy one, nevertheless. Deacon* KINDMAN *has evidently followed his plan to the letter. Everybody that he invited is present, and a few that he did not, have happened in. The company have just risen from prayer with the good old-style preacher, who has thoroughly appreciated and improved the now unusual opportunity. He takes this occasion to combine two sermons — one on Thanksgiving Day, and one on Christmas—which have for many years been growing in his heart, waiting for a chance to be preached.*

Deacon KINDMAN.
Now in tuneful chorus, our thanks we will prolong,
And sing to the Father of fathers our own thanksgiving song.
With soul, as well as larynx, let all of us rejoice,
And not perform our worship entirely with the voice.

[JEREMIAH, *a neighboring poor man's son, passes round papers containing a hymn, which he has copied in an uncultured but very readable hand.*

All sing.

HYMN OF THANKSGIVING.

To the air, "Portuguese Hymn."

We thank thee, O Father, for all that is bright—
The gleam of the day, and the stars of the night;
The flowers of our youth, and the fruits of our prime,
And blessings e'er marching the path-way of time.

We thank thee, O Father, for all that is drear—
The sob of the tempest—the flow of the tear;
For never in blindness, and never in vain,
Thy mercy permitted a sorrow or pain.

We thank thee, O Father, for song and for feast—
The harvest that glowed, and the wealth that increased;
For never a blessing encompassed thy child,
But thou in thy mercy looked downward and smiled.

We thank thee, O Father of all! for the power
Of aiding each other in life's darkest hour;
The generous heart and the bountiful hand,
And all the soul-help that sad souls understand.

We thank thee, O Father! for days yet to be—
For hopes that our future will call us to thee;
That all our Eternity form, through thy love,
One Thanksgiving Day in the mansions above.

Deacon KINDMAN.
And now a neighbor's daughter, who—don't waste time to doubt—
Knows how to read a poem, and turn it inside out,
Who first sits down and invites it into her heart and soul,
And part of herself surrenders entire to its control,

And part of her mind keeps clear, like, when ready, as she ought
To be—to give to the author the aid of her own clear thought
(For face and form and gesture—be 't good or be it bad—
Add much to an author's meaning, or rob him of what he had);

Third Chain.

Whose mental frills and tuckers are laid upon the shelf,
And who, in her well-conned subject, can partly forget herself;
This daughter of my good neighbor, who sits, himself, near by,
And needn't be blamed for looking at her with a partial eye;

Will read a poem to us, presenting, I believe,
A legend of what happened on the first Christmas eve.
    ALICE (*the neighbor's daughter, reads, plainly, thoughtfully, spiritedly, and without affectation*):

THE VOICE OF A STAR; OR, THE FIRST CHRISTMAS EVE.

    Dark Night once more her tent unfurled
      On Power's first-century home—
    Upon the marble heart of the world—
      The great, grand city of Rome;
    And hushed at last were the chariot-tires,
      And still the sandalled feet,
    And dimmed the palace-window-fires
      On many a noble street;
    And to a roof a maiden came,
      With eyes as angels love,
    And looked up at the spheres of flame
      That softly gleamed above.

    She gazed at them with a misty eye,
      And spoke, in accents sad:
    "O tell me, gold-birds of the sky
      (If ever a voice you had!),
    Is justice dull from a palsy stroke,
      And deaf, as well as blind?
    Else why must e'er the heaviest yoke
      Be placed on womankind?
    Why should the solace of man's heart
      Be oft his meanest slave?
    Why is her life e'er torn apart
      By those she has toiled to save?

    "Why should the mould of the human race
      Be crushed and thrown away,

Whenever it lacks the outward grace
    That wooes the stronger clay?
Why must the mothers of men be bought
    And sold, like beasts that die?
Why are they scourged, for little or naught,
    And barred of all reply?
Why are we women of Rome e'er told
    That we should happy be,
Because not kept like flocks in fold,
    Like those across the sea?

"Have we no heart? Have we no mind?
    Must not our conscience speak?
Say! must our souls be dumb or blind,
    Because our hands are weak?
Must we be ever the laughing-stock
    Of man's fond, fickle heart?
Were we but born for Fate to mock—
    To play a menial part?
Must all our triumphs be a lie—
    Our joys in fetters clad?
O tell me, gold-birds of the sky
    (If ever a voice you had!)."

Then from the east, a new, bright star
    Flashed to her flashing eye,
And seemed to speak to her from afar,
    With courteous, kind reply:
"Why weep, fair maid, upon the eve
    Of Victory's coming morn?
It is o'er-strange for one to grieve,
    Whose champion's to be born!
To-morrow a new, old king appears,
    With dimpled, mighty hand;
And He shall reign a million years,
    O'er many a princely land.

"His mother a queen the world shall see,
    Whose reign doth e'er endure;

All women shall his sisters be,
  Whose ways are just and pure;
A woman's fault shall not be her death,
  By men or angels seen;
Repentance, and His God-strewn breath,
  May always step between.
A woman's fame, by merit won,
  Shall add to her queenly grace;
And higher, as the years march on,
  Shall be her destined place.

"And four great words the world shall see
  Enwoven with man's life:
Mother and sister two shall be,
  And two be daughter and wife.
It shall be felt that she whose care
  The lamp of thrift makes burn,
Can take with him an equal share
  Of all their lives may earn;
That she whose soft and healing hand
  Can soothe, with blessing bright,
Is no less great and true and grand,
  Than he who leads the fight."

Like one who through the woods may grope
  Till light comes to his eyes,
The maiden thrilled with new-born hope,
  And seized the glad surprise.
The voice of the star she understood;
  Its glorious meaning knew;
And all her dreams of woman's good
  Seemed likely to come true.
And when once more the twilight gray
  Was brightened by the morn,
Within a manger far away,
  The infant Christ was born.

  [*All the ladies present applaud vigorously. The men
    nod, in mild approbation. The old clergyman*

states that he has a series of thirteen sermons upon the subject of womanhood's Christian ennoblement, which he should be glad to give in the district school-house, or in any church where the people would like to assemble for the purpose of hearing him. Deacon KINDMAN *arranges with him to preach the first of the series in his parlor, upon the following Sunday evening. All present declare they will come. The company then sing "Nearer, my God, to Thee."*

Deacon KINDMAN (*holding the hymn-book in his hand*).
Not alone in the country, where God's first work was done,
Is found the true religion that came from His mighty Son;
Hear what an author's fancy heard a city brother say
When just about to be "moving," upon the First of May.

[*A small orphaned boy, whose residence just now is the neighboring poor-house, and who, even in that environment, has developed wonderful taste and talent, recites:*

THE OLD HYMN-BOOK.

Yes, wife, we're going to move once more;
   The last time, I declare,
Until the everlasting shore
   Sends word it wants us there!
Some things this time with us we'll take,
   Some leave here in disgust,
And some we'll lose, and some we'll break,
   As movers always must.
The family Bible we will find
   Devoutly carried through;
But also, wife, don't fail to mind
   And save the hymn-book, too!

Though finger-marked and cupboard-worn,
   And shabby in its looks,

Third Chain.

I prize that volume, soiled and torn,
    Next to the Book of books;
When David trimmed his golden lyre
    With song forget-me-nots,
He left a flame of sacred fire
    For Wesley and for Watts.
And many other singers, wife,
    Have made God's glory known
In hymns and tunes that drew their life
    From echoes round the throne!

I've sung them when, on lofty track,
    My heart soared through the sky,
And every word and tone brought back
    A telegraph-reply;
I've hummed them when my soul with grief
    Feared all its prayers were vain,
Till they have braced up my belief,
    And soothed my doubting-pain;
I've told them to the woods, and stirred
    The trees up to rejoice;
I've joined in meetings where God heard
    Ten thousand in one voice!

I've paused—those sacred words to hear—
    When life was gay and bright,
And every sound that charmed the ear
    Brought glory to the sight;
I've heard them when the sexton's spade
    Had cut my life in two,
And my sad heart, by their sweet aid,
    Has walked the valley through.
Ah, wife! when heaven's great music-burst
    Awakes my senses dim,
I humbly hope they'll give me first
    A good old-fashioned hymn!

I trust, when our last moving-day
    Has shown us God's good love,

And we have settled down to stay
   In colonies above,
We'll find a hundred earthly things
   Our hearts had twined about,
And which—so tight the memory clings—
   Heaven wouldn't be heaven without;
And somewhere, in that blessèd place,
   God grant I may behold,
Near by the precious word of grace,
   My hymn-book, bound in gold!

[*A great deal of appreciation is expressed of the reading of this poem. No one seems much struck by the subject-matter, except the old clergyman, who remarks that he has a series of fourteen sermons upon the influence of hymns on the human race, which he will be happy to give at the school-house, or any other place where an audience will assemble to hear them. Deacon* KINDMAN *makes arrangements to have the first of the series delivered in his parlor, upon the ensuing Thursday evening, and all the company promise to be present, if possible.*]

Deacon KINDMAN.
And now our good old pastor, whose heart is ever alive
To other good old pastors, and how they toil and strive,
Will read that a city preacher, with fame in his well-filled hand,
Became as little children, when near to the heavenly land.
   The old CLERGYMAN *reads:*

THE PASTOR'S FAREWELL.*

The sermon was o'er—the prayer—the song—
   And dimmed was the mellow light;
With Summer at heart, the homeward throng
   Went out in the Winter night.

---

* An incident that occurred during Henry Ward Beecher's last Sunday evening in the church where he had preached so many years.

But the pastor stayed, at his tired heart's choice,
  To list to the chanted word;
For the organ-loft and the human voice
  Still sung to the pastor's Lord.

The sweet tones brought to his wearied heart
  Their mingled smiles and tears;
And he felt that night full loath to part
  From the shrine of forty years.

The scene of a thousand wondrous hours
  He saw as he glanced around;
The vase of affection's faithful flowers—
  The blood of a battle-ground.

'Twas here he had preached with tones of love,
  Or the clarion call of strife,
Of God within, as well as above;
  And sweetened the bread of life.

And here, with gesture of brave command,
  And tenderly beaming face,
He reached to the world a thrilling hand,
  And fought for the human race.

'Twas here, with a strength by anguish bought,
  And a love that never slept,
He rocked the cradle of new-born thought,
  While the century smiled and wept.

He saw the thousands that o'er this track
  Had walked to the country of day;
And now they seemed to be reaching back,
  And beckoning him away.

But ere long time his soul had been
  By olden memories stirred,
Two children softly wandered in,
  To list to the chanted word.

Two young, fresh hearts, with a goodly sum
    Of Innocence' saving leaven,
Like such it is said ours must become
    Before we can enter heaven.

They heard in silence, with face upturned,
    And tremulous, deep surprise,
And all the fire of the music burned
    Within their youthful eyes!

There crept to the old man's eyes a mist;
    And down the pulpit stair
He gently came, and tenderly kissed
    The children lingering there;

And o'er their shoulders his arms he threw,
    This king with the crown of gray:
And finally, like three comrades true,
    Together they walked away.

And two went out in the Winter night,
    Their earth-toil just begun;
The other, forth to eternal light—
    His work for the planet done.

———

SCENE III., *the same; it has been growing dark, and is nearly time to go home. The remainder of the afternoon has passed in recitations, songs, and speeches, and all seem, upon the whole, to have had a good time.*

 Deacon KINDMAN.
And now let's be reminded that though Misfortune's hand
Has reached us all for reasons that God can understand,
While we, short-sighted creatures, shrink murmuring from its touch,
Yet there are those who suffer a thousand times as much.

  [*Enter an elocutionist, dressed as a tramp. His face has a lonely, haggard look; his eyes are cast down-*

"AND O'ER THEIR SHOULDERS HIS ARMS HE THREW."

Third Chain.

ward, with occasional furtive glances at those before him; his look of grim distress is assumed so naturally that some of the company think at first that he is a real tramp. He recites:

THE CONVICT'S CHRISTMAS EVE.

The term was done; my penalty was past;
I saw the outside of the walls at last.
When I left that stone punishment of sin,
'Twas 'most as hard as when I first went in.
It seemed at once as though the sweet-voiced air
Told slanderous tales about me everywhere;
As if the ground itself was shrinking back
For fear 'twould get the Cain's mark of my track.
Women would edge away, with shrewd she-guesses,
As if my very glance would spoil their dresses;
Men looked me over with close, careless gaze,
And understood my downcast, jail-bird ways;
My hands were so grim-hardened and defiled,
I wouldn't have had the cheek to pet a child;
If I had spoken to a dog that day,
He would have tipped his nose and walked away.
And so I wandered in a jail of doubt,
Whence neither heaven nor earth would let me out.
The world itself seemed to me every bit
As hard a prison as the one I'd quit.

If you are made of anything but dirt,
If you've a soul that other souls can hurt,
Turn to the right henceforth, whoever passes:
It's death to drop among the lawless classes!
Men lose, who lose the friendship of the law,
A blessing from each breath of air they draw;
They know th' advantage of a good square face,
When theirs has been disfigured by disgrace!

So I trudged round, appropriately slow
For one with no particular place to go;

The houses scowled and stared as if to say,
"You jail-bird, we are honest; walk away!"
The factories seemed to scream, when I came near,
"Stand back! unsentenced men are working here!"
And virtue had th' appearance, all the time,
Of trying hard to push me back to crime.

It struck me strange, that stormy, snow-bleached day,
To watch the different people on the way,
All carrying parcels, of all sorts of sizes,
As carefully as gold and silver prizes.
Well-dressed or poor—I could not understand
Why each one hugged a bundle in his hand.
I asked an old policeman what it meant:
He looked me over, with eyes shrewdly bent,
While muttering, in a voice that fairly froze,
"It's 'cause to-morrow's Christmas, I suppose."
And then the fact came crashing over me,
How horribly alone a man can be!

I don't pretend what tortures yet may wait
For souls that have not run their reckonings straight;
It isn't for mortal ignorance to say
What kind of night may follow any day;
There may be pain for sin some time found out,
That sin on earth knows nothing yet about;
But I don't think there's any harbor known
Worse for a wrecked soul—than to be Alone.
Alone! there maybe never has occurred
A word whose gloom is gloomier than that word!

You who can brighten up your Christmas joys
With all affection's small but mighty toys,
Who fancy that your gifts of love be rash,
And presents are not worth their price in cash,
Thank God, with love and thrift no more at war,
That you've some one to spend your money for!
A dollar plays a very dingy part
Till magnetized by some one's grateful heart.

"AN OPEN CHURCH SOME LOOK OF WELCOME WORE;"

Third Chain.

So evening saw me straggling up and down
Within the gayly lighted, desolate town,
A hungry, sad heart-hermit all the while,
My rough face begging for a friendly smile.
Folks talked with folks, in new-made warmth and glee,
But no one had a word or look for me;
Love flowed like water, but it could not make
The world forgive me for my one mistake.

An open church some look of welcome wore;
I crept in soft, and sat down near the door.
I'd never seen, 'mongst my unhappy race,
So many happy children in one place;
I never knew how much a hymn could bring
From Heaven, until I heard those children sing;
I never saw such sweet-breathed gales of glee,
As swept around that fruitful Christmas-tree!

You who have tripped through childhood's merry days
With passionate love protecting all your ways,
Who did not see a Christmas-time go by
Without some present for your sparkling eye,
Thank God, whose goodness gave such joy its birth,
And scattered heaven-seeds in the dust of earth!
In stone-paved ground my thorny field was set:
I never had a Christmas present yet.

And so I sat and saw them, and confess
Felt all th' unhappier for their happiness;
And when a man gets into such a state,
He's very proud—or very desolate.

Just then a cry of "Fire!" amongst us came;
The pretty Christmas-tree was all aflame;
And one sweet child there in our startled gaze
Was screaming, with her white clothes all ablaze!

The crowd seemed crazy-like, both old and young,
And very slow of deed, though swift of tongue.

But one knew what to do, and not to say,
And he a convict, just let loose that day.

I fought like one who deals in deadly strife:
I wrapped my life around that child's sweet life;
I choked the flames that choked her, with rich cloaks,
Stol'n from some good but very frightened folks;
I gave the dear girl to her parents' sight,
Unharmed by anything excepting fright;
I tore the blazing branches from the tree;
Till all was safe, and no one hurt but me.

That night, of which I asked for sleep in vain—
That night, that tossed me round on prongs of pain,
That stabbed me with fierce tortures through and through—
Was still the happiest that I ever knew.
I felt that I at last had earned a place
Among my race, by suffering for my race;
I felt the glorious facts wouldn't let me miss
A mother's thanks—perhaps a child's sweet kiss;
That man's warm gratitude would find a plan
To lift me up, and help me be a man.

Next day they brought a letter to my bed;
I opened it with tingling nerves, and read:
"You have upon my kindness certain claims,
For rescuing my young child from the flames;
Such deeds deserve a hand unstained by crime;
I trust you will reform while yet there's time.
The blackest sinner may find mercy still.
(Enclosed please find a thousand-dollar bill.)
Our paths of course on different roads must lie;
Don't follow me for any more. Good-by."

I scorched the dirty rag till it was black;
Enclosed it in a rag, and sent it back.

That very night, I cracked a tradesman's door,
Stole with my blistered hands ten thousand more,

Third Chain.

Which I next day took special pains to send
To my good, distant, wealthy, high-toned friend,
And wrote upon it in a steady hand,
In words I hoped he wouldn't misunderstand:
"Money is cheap, as I have shown you here;
But gratitude and sympathy are dear.
These rags are stolen—have been—may often be:
I trust the one wasn't that you sent to me.
Hoping your pride and you are reconciled—
From the black, sinful rescuer of your child."

I crept to court—a crushed, triumphant worm—
Confessed the theft, and took another term.

My life closed, and began; and I went back
Among the rogues that walk the broad-gauged track.
I prowl 'mid every sort of sin that's known;
I walk rough roads—but do not walk *Alone*.

> [*Company take leave of their host, and disperse, cheerfully but thoughtfully, with the consciousness of having had a splendid time, but with pity in their hearts for those who are more miserable than Poverty could possibly make them.*

FOURTH CHAIN.

Fourth Chain.

I.

In the last quarter of this century—
This grand, electric-lighted century—
This steam-propelled, far-speaking century—
That called the idle vapors to their work,
Made giants of them, gave them arms of steel,
And made them toil ere to their sport returned—
That caught the fire-fly lightnings on the wing,
And caged them into lamps that kill the dark—
Century that confirms the Arabian Nights—
Century with the blossom and the fruit
Of eons that have grown through tears and blood—
Century to be quoted as that one
Wherein Man first declared by deed that he
Was emperor of all the elements;
This quick-nerved, high-strung nineteenth century,
That found new hideous ways for War to use
In killing, and thus made Peace fashionable;
This century that soon, with toll of bell,
And trumpet-peal, and boom of brazen gun,
And shouts of men, half joyful and half sad,
Shall close its clanging gate for evermore—

It is not strange that we should wonder oft
What legends maybe will be told of us
In the strange, silent century next to come.

In the new, waiting years so soon to come—
When boys that now sport laughing in the streets

Shall be grave grandsires, wondering at the glee
Of frivolous boys, and making dividends
With their grim silent partner—Rheumatism;
When tiny girls, now perching on our knees,
Become old ladies, dignified and prim;
When "Eighteen hundred" shall a memory be,
And "Nineteen hundred" sound like old friends' names—
Perchance the children may some legends hear
Of this last quarter of this century:

Tell them of Grant's too-soon pathetic death.
How the old chief so silently encamped
In the King-city—two long mournful days,
And the weird mournful nights that flitted round;
How past his solemn bed sad thousands marched
To see him, ere the coverlid was drawn
O'er his pale face forever; how at last
His great black hearse crept up the broad highway
'Twixt marble palaces thick cloaked in crape,
And crowded close with hushed and bowing forms;
How clans that late had sought each other's blood
Now arm in arm marched with the conqueror;
And how the requiem guns that greeted him
At his half-made but some day gorgeous tent
Shook not the city more than did its grief.

Tell this to them—although may be forgotten
Amid the century's whirl—this funeral-song:

THE CAPTAIN IS ASLEEP.

Let the muffled drums mourn
    Heavy and deep,
And flags with crape be borne:
    The Captain is asleep.
On a hushed and solemn bed,
    Alone he lies.
Tender words of him are said,

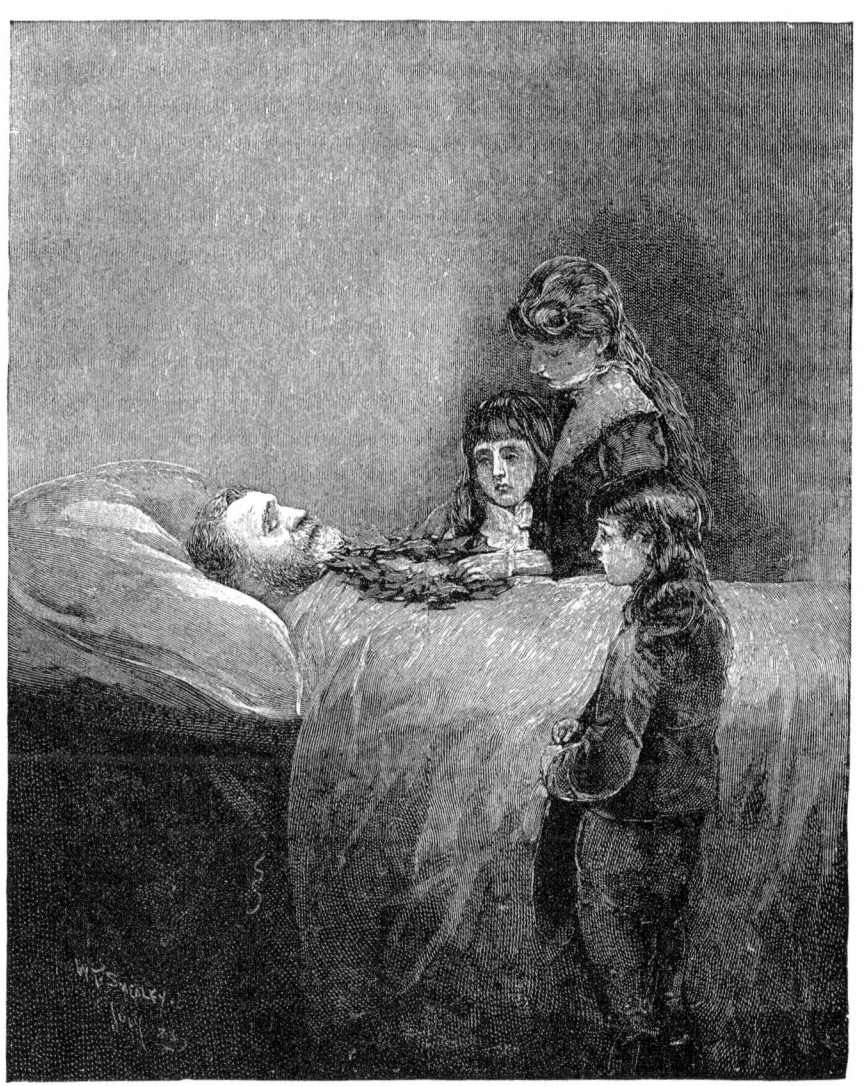

"TENDER WORDS OF HIM ARE SAID."

Fourth Chain.

There are waiting for his hands
Love bouquets from many lands;
   But he will not rise.

Never in his childhood days
   Such slumber came;
Nor ere war's electric blaze
   Streamed o'er his name,
When, through eyes with watching dim,
His young mother bent o'er him,
Wreathing hopes upon his brow,
Did he sleep so well as now.

Let the silver horns trail
   Anthems that weep:
Let them voice the early tale
   Of the Captain asleep;
Tell the struggles that he knew
Ere his life-work stood in view,
And the clouds that vexed his eyes
Ere his star flashed through the skies.

Men, you must his mourners be,
   For he was brave.
Harvester of courage, he
   Knew when to save.
Cruel as the tiger's fang
   Until war was done,
He would soothe the smallest pang
   When the strife was won.
Only death could conquer him,
And his fight with that was grim.
As in his best days of pride,
Hero to the last he died.

Women, holy in his eyes
Was the pureness that you prize.
Palaces round him had smiled,
Kingly shows his days beguiled;

But he loved and sought release,
    Turned from lofty spire and dome,
Came for comfort and for peace
    To the fireside of his home.

Fame, you have done your best
For the Warrior of the West,
Who, with grand, heroic rush,
    Reached your regions at a leap.
Sound his praise again!—but hush!
    The Captain is asleep.
Slumbering early; but 'tis best
That the weary man should rest.
He has had the care and strife,
Ten times over, of a life.

Grief, you came when Rest
    Should have thrown her spell—
You were of rare barbs possessed—
    Oh, you pierced him well!
It is brave to fall and die
    With an arrow in the heart;
It is noble, great, and high
    To live and bear its smart.
Sound so grand was never heard
As is pain without a word.

Let the drums cease to mourn—
    Let the clouds break;
Let the badge of grief be torn;
    The Captain is awake!
Warriors brave in yonder land,
    Who once lingered here,
Grasp our Chieftain by the hand,
    Give him friendly cheer!

II.

Or tell them of the fair ambassadress
That France—hot-veined republic of the East—

Sent to her sister of the Western waves
Bearing the magic torch of liberty:
France—she who with her aid long years ago,
Gave us the eagle—type of Victory:

THE VESTAL.

Into the bay—the great, wide, wealth-fringed bay,
    Whose every tide sweeps hamlets to our shores—
Where king-slaves have their fetters struck away—
    Whence can be read, on the new nation's doors,
"Leave hopelessness behind, who enters here!"
Harbor of hope!—invaded, without fear,
By ships of labor, sailed from rotting ports,
And toil whose plumage had been stol'n by courts—
Into that bay, a virgin-guest comes nigh,
And holds her lamp unto the star-gemmed sky.

They sent her from that empire of the East,
    Whose "king" hath dynasty the same as ours;
From the rich harvest, and the vineyard-feast;
    From glistening domes, and ivy-mantled towers.
Peasants have toiled, throughout the sultry day,
The tributes of her ocean-march to pay;
The artisan has wrought, that she might rise
And smile into his western brother's eyes;
The thought-smith—he with busy heart and brain—
Helped feed her torch that gleams across the main.*

She brings to us a century that is past;
    The legend of a gift of long agone;
A favor that like diamonds shall last,
    And gleam but brighter as the years gloom on.
They gave us gold when recompense was doubt;
Perish the greed that blots that memory out!
They gave us hope, when our own star had set;
May the brain soften that would shun the debt!

---

* Nearly all classes of the French people contributed toward the cost of sending us Bartholdi's Statue of Liberty.

They gave us heroes, with a fame as bright
As mountain watch-fires on a winter's night.

Stand, Vestal, with thy virgin flame e'er clear,
    And guard our future pilgrims to their rest
In the great city, where, year after year,
    Their march shall feed our never-failing West.
Tell those who hated greed, and hurried thence,
That honest toil hath here a recompense;
Say to the lawless—whosoe'er they be—
That men must live obedient, to live free;
And sing for us, o'er the blue waves' expanse—
"With all our faults and thine, we love thee, France!"

III.

Or tell them of the years when our long coast
Lay prosperous, but defenceless; all that while
That other nations blotted the free sky
With the black plumage of their war-ships' smoke;
And our Unbuilt Ship sang a gloomy song
And strove to rouse the nation's fear and pride:

SONG OF THE UNBUILT SHIP.

They were making me a king of the sea,
    The ocean's pride and fear;
But ere I was done the world moved on,
    And left me stranded here—
To the world's sharp eyes an enterprise
    That ere it was tested failed;
A ruin low that was always so,
    A wreck that has ne'er been sailed.
I sit and cower 'neath many an hour
    That drearily drifts to me;
But visions have they from far away,
    And these are the sights I see:

"A WRECK THAT HAS NE'ER BEEN SAILED."

Fourth Chain.

Grim men who toil at blades that spoil,
    In populous far-off lands;
And murderer-guns that Art's rough sons
    Mould hot in their giant hands;
Steel diggers of graves, that walk the waves,
    And rule with their rude alarms,
Or cripple and kill with close-eyed skill,
    And long, invisible arms.
Oh, a wondrous shower of godlike power
    This grand decade can boast:
But what if it frown on shipping and town
    Of a long, defenceless coast?

For the great star-ships now suffer eclipse
    That were from the forest born,
And boats that have birth in the mines of earth
    Are laughing us all to scorn.
The nation that gave to the watchful wave
    Its swift and strongest guest,
With triumph is done, and her ocean-sun
    Stands low in the blushing west.
O world just made, your grandeur is weighed,
    Your treasuries all men know;
But why should you seek a wealth too weak
    To guard you against a foe?

You may gild your domes and adorn your homes,
    Proud men of the Rich New Land;
But what are they worth if half the earth
    Is fired by a war's red brand?
The watchmen sleep of the banks that keep
    A continent's wealth in store:
Say, where are your locks when an enemy knocks
    With clenched hand at the door?
Your daughters and wives, whose winsome lives
    Make every land more fair—
What have you, then, O thoughtless men,
    To guard them from despair?

I see bright gold into tablets rolled;
    I see iron leagues of ore:
Rouse up with a zeal for the nation's weal,
    And carry them to the shore!
The power to defend holds many a friend;
    Force oft shows clear the right;
The surest lease of comfort and peace
    Is a sturdy strength to fight.
Let walls of iron your treasurers environ,
    As well as of heart and brain;
Shun heedless guilt! and the ship unbuilt
    May not have sung in vain.

IV.

Or tell them of the hideous, creeping beast,
That trailed its slime along our grandest walks,
That named a million kings Laöcoon,
That twined around the fairest and the best,
And crushed them in its anaconda-coils;
That crept into our homes, and not content
With driving mortals from their Paradise,
Would make even that a hell.

THE SERPENT OF THE STILL.

The tempter, as God's legends tell—
    Allowed on earth to roam—
Crushed that which Woman loves so well,
    Her sweet and sacred home.
From Eden, lost through his black art,
    She wandered out forlorn;
She cursed him in her gentle heart
    With meek but deadly scorn.
And since, in varied guise of sin,
    He works his hateful will,
And reappears to-day within
    The serpent of the still.

"HE TWINES ABOUT HER TREMBLING LIFE."

Fourth Chain.

He comes not now in subtle mood—
    With smiles, as long ago—
Enticing her by honeyed food,
    And mysteries she may know;
He makes insulting, swift advance
    Into her bright home-nest,
Admitted and embraced, perchance,
    By those she loves the best.
He brings the world where he must dwell,
    Her days and nights to fill,
Transmuting Paradise to Hell—
    This serpent of the still!

He twines about her trembling life,
    And soils it with his slime;
He fills the hours with foolish strife,
    He sows the seeds of crime.
And Poverty and fierce Disease,
    And Hunger and Disgrace,
And Death by death-empanged degrees,
    Are in his cold embrace.
To grieve, to hurt, to rend, to smite,
    To ruin, and to kill,
Are leaden links of his delight—
    The serpent of the still!

Rouse, woman, in your quiet power,
    Your heart's man-withering frown,
Your hand that rules the festal hour,
    And crush the monster down!
You shape the human form and soul,
    You mark the infant's way,
Youth's fancy you can oft control,
    Man's action you can sway:
Bend every blessing of your life
    To fight its deadliest ill!
Strike—daughter, maiden, widow, wife—
    This serpent of the still!

FIFTH CHAIN.

Fifth Chain.

SCENE, *a club-room. Enter two decayed poets, with several manuscripts which have been submitted to them for consideration. They seat themselves solemnly at a table, and proceed to open court.*

SMYTHERRES (*one of the decayed poets*).
My colleague in poetic emperorhood,
   I deem it best that we discourse in rhyme;
   In the set sonnet* of the olden time;
Miltonic sonnet; for 'tis well and good,
That we, who might surpass him if we would
   (Our predecessors o'er him used to climb),
   Should let our strains his modest voice o'er-chime;
Though we ourselves are still misunderstood,
Excepting by ourselves and by each other,
   And people will not read the things we write,
Unless we ask them to—a precious bother!—
   Yet we in criticism can vent some spite,

---

* The English sonnet, so far as I have been able to observe, consists, as such, principally of being composed of fourteen lines—rhymed partly under a certain rule, and partly according to the fancy or ability of the author. The great danger in undertaking it seems rarely to have been escaped: that of paying so much attention to the rhymes that the sense and sentiment are neglected. Among the happy exceptions to this unhappy rule are Milton and Shakespeare, who sometimes say more in the compactness of their sonnets even than in some of their more inflated forms. But there is a singular difference between their rhyming methods: Milton following the intricate Italian style, while Shakespeare, in that direct, slashing way with which he goes about everything, simply rhymes alternate lines, finishes up with a rhymed couplet, and so makes an end of it. It strikes me that the two senile poets who appear in the accompanying pages, in selecting models after whom to chipper away at each other, have chosen two good representative sonneteers of the English language, and — imitator-like — made a bad mess of it.

And rivals' praises with our venom smother.
So ope these efforts to our suffering sight.

    JOHNNES (*the other decayed poet*).
That we discourse in sonnets, I consent;
    Though from myself, dear brother, please to ask
Shakespearian rhyme.—So I have precedent,
    My style is proper.—Let us to the task.
Of manuscripts this package doth consist,
    Which we must now examine, and decide
Whether they have our license to exist,
    Or whether they in failure must abide.
Ah me!—a great responsibility
    It is, to say what shall and shall not live
In literature and art—especially,
    When some survive, for all the pains we give.
Draw forth the first presumer that doth wait,
And let us seal the verdict of his fate.

    SMYTHERRES (*opening a package*).
I know not whether it were best to give
    These lines within our time and thought a place;
    They discourse of a non-poetic race;
Who, though of course we must permit to live,
Are mostly ignorant and primitive;
    Therefore the title shows, upon its face,
    An utter lack of true poetic grace.
But let us shake it in our critic-sieve;
For *some* opinion must be renderèd
    On all the manuscripts we are receiving,
And we have been accused oft-times, 'tis said,
    Of thoughtless, half-malicious judgment giving;
Therefore these lines shall every word be read
    (Besides, too, that's the way we make our living).
    Reads:

THE NEGRO FUNERAL.

I was walking in Savannah, past a church decayed and dim,
When there slowly through the window came a plaintive funeral hymn;

AND HE SAID: "NOW DON' BE WEEPIN' FOR DIS PRETTY BIT O' CLAY."

And a sympathy awakened, and a wonder quickly grew,
Till I found myself environed in a little negro pew.

Out at front a colored couple sat in sorrow, nearly wild;
On the altar was a coffin, in the coffin was a child.
I could picture him when living—curly hair, protruding lip—
And had seen perhaps a thousand in my hurried Southern trip.

But no baby ever rested in the soothing arms of Death
That had fanned more flames of sorrow with his little fluttering breath;
And no funeral ever glistened with more sympathy profound
Than was in the chain of tear-drops that enclasped those mourners round.

Rose a sad old colored preacher at the little wooden desk—
With a manner grandly awkward, with a countenance grotesque;
With simplicity and shrewdness on his Ethiopian face;
With the ignorance and wisdom of a crushed, undying race.

And he said: "Now don' be weepin' for dis pretty bit o' clay—
For de little boy who lived dere, he done gone an' run away!
He was doin' very fine here, an' he 'preciate your love;
But his sure 'nuff Father want him in de large house up above.

"Now He didn' give you dat baby, by a hundred thousan' mile!
He just think you need some sunshine, an' He lend it for a while!
An' He let you keep an' love it, till your hearts was bigger grown;
An' dese silver tears you're sheddin's jest de interest on de loan.

"Here yer oder pretty chilrun!—don't be makin' it appear
Dat your love got sort o' 'nop'lized by dis little fellow here;
Don' pile up too much your sorrow on deir little mental shelves,
So's to kind o' set 'em wonderin' if dey're no account demselves!

"Just you think, you poor deah mounahs, creepin' 'long o'er Sorrow's way,
What a blessèd little picnic dis yere baby's got to-day!
His gran'faders an' gran'moders crowd de little fellow round
In de angel-tended garden of de Big Plantation Ground.

"An' dey ask him, 'Was your feet sore?' an' take off his little
    shoes,
An' dey wash him, an' dey kiss him, an' dey say, 'Now what's de
    news?'
An' de Lawd done cut his tongue loose; den de little fellow say,
'All our folks down in de valley tries to keep de hebbenly way.'

"An' his eyes dey brightly sparkle at de pretty things he view;
Den a tear come, an' he whisper, 'But I want my paryents, too!'
But de Angel Chief Musician teach dat boy a little song:
Says, 'If only dey be fait'ful dey will soon be comin' 'long.'

"An' he'll get an education dat will proberbly be worth
Seberal times as much as any you could buy for him on earth;
He'll be in de Lawd's big school-house, widout no contempt or fear;
While dere's no end to de bad t'ings might have happened to him
    here.

"So, my pooah dejected mounahs, let your hearts wid Jesus rest,
An' don' go to critercisin' dat ar One w'at knows de best!
He have sent us many comforts—He have right to take away—
To de Lawd be praise an' glory now and ever!—Let us pray."

JOHNNES.
What horrid taste! what disregard of rules!
    To pick up such a story as this one,
And voice it! where are our poetic schools,
    When such absurd things can be safely done?
The proper subjects for poetic flights,
    Are clouds, stars, skies, courts, tournaments, and kings,
And sickly love-tales.—We must set to rights
    A state of things which tolerates such things.
Let's give that author such a verbal basting
    That he will never dare again to show
His head in printed letters, after tasting
    The cup of our acidulated woe.
To think that pen and type should be defiled
Upon the funeral of a negro child!

SMYTHERRES.
And dialect—foe to poetic speech—
  Appears here, in this undeserving verse,
  And if 'twere possible, would make it worse.
Its growing prevalence mankind should teach,
That when an author downward thus doth reach,
  He should incur the critic's hottest curse—
  His Pegasus being harnessed to his hearse;
And though the lines of some good writers preach
That th' exact language men and women use
  Is proper, when their ideas you're expressing,
Yet 'tis what we prefer to have our views,
  That dialect is an improper dressing.
Shakespeare, Burns, Dante, Homer, if you choose—
  Had lapses of the same—but 'twas distressing!
      [*Sighs deeply, opens another manuscript, and reads:*

THE FOUR TRAVELLERS.

They were telling their experience—just a small band of that race
Whose religion oft illumines e'en the darkness of the face;
Whose true fancy passes limits that cold reason can not reach;
Whose expressions are more accurate for the rudeness of their speech.
And they drew their illustrations—not from ancient lore profound—
But from nineteenth-century wonders, that are scattered all around.

And one said: "I'm goin' to hebben in de row-boat ob God's grace;
An' I'm pullin' mighty lively, for to win de hebbenly race."
But the leader said: "Be keerful; for de arm ob flesh may fail,
An' de oars may break—or danger may come ridin' on de gale;
An' be sure you make dat boat large; for no Christian ken affo'd
To say 'No' to any helpah who desires to step abo'd."

And one said: "I'm goin' to hebben in de sail-boat ob de word;
An' my faith it stitched de canvas, an' my breeze is from de Lord
An' my craft it foam de watahs, as I speed upon my way,
'Till it seems like I was makin' 'bout a hundr'd miles a day."
But the leader said: "Be watchful; work an' struggle more an' more;
Look for lots o' calms a-comin'—look for breakers on de shore!"

And one rose and said: "*I'm* trabellin' in de steamboat ob God's power,
An' it seems like I was makin' 'bout a hundred knots an hour!
An' my berth is all done paid for—an' my d'rection all is known,
Till our gospel steamer whistles for her landin' near de throne!"
And the leader said: "Be earnest; you jus' watch, an' toil, an' pray,
Les' yer engine bu'st its boiler, an' you shipwreck on de way."

Then a poor old woman rose up—bent and haggard, worn and weak—
And she leaned upon her crutches, and her tongue was slow to speak;
And she said: "I up an' started moah dan fifty yeahs ago—
Started off *afoot* for hebben—an' de journey's mighty slow!
Dere was streams dat had no bridges—dere was stone-hills for to climb—
Dere was swamps an' stubs an' briers waitin' for me all de time;

"Dere was clouds ob persecution, full ob thunder an' cold rain—
Dere was any 'mount ob wanderin', dere was woes I couldn't explain;
Dere was folks dat 'fore I asked 'em, my poor waverin' footsteps showed
Into country dat was pleasant, but dat didn't contain de Road;
But de Lawd, he fin'lly tol' me, when I'm boun' to have de way,
An' I think perhaps I'm makin' maybe half a mile a day."

Then the leader said: "Dere's nothin' 'gainst de rapid transit plan—
Jus' you get to hebben, my bredren, any honest way you can!
If you folks kin sail to glory, I don' know but dat's all right!
But I can not help believin'—if we all should die to-night—
When you boatmen land in Canaan, wid some narrow 'scapes to tell,
You'd fin' dat ol' sister waitin', wid her feet all washed an' well!"

JOHNNES.
Ignorant rhymester! delver 'mongst the clods!
  Why should he choose such undeserving themes?
Why can't he take stars, angels, demons, gods,
  And other subjects fit for poets' dreams?
Why doesn't he hint what can not be expressed?*

---

* "There is no poetry higher than that which by its expression hints at a wealth of aspiration, desire, yearning, that is unexpressed because inexpressible."—[FROM A RECENT BOOK REVIEW.]

Fifth Chain.

Why doesn't he aim at what he ne'er can see?
Yearn for what wouldn't be known if 'twere possessed—
  Aspire to what he knows can never be?
Or why not write as you do?—rake the past
  For fancies that in others' minds have grown—
See that they are in proper measure cast—
  Then cheerfully exploit them as his own?
    SMYTHERRES (*angrily*).
You are a thief yourself!
    JOHNNES.
            A robber, you!

  SMYTHERRES.
Knave!
    JOHNNES.
        Plagiarist!
  SMYTHERRES.
            Emasculated shrew!

> [*They pummel each other rhythmically, with the remaining manuscripts. One of them* flies open, and reveals still another dialect poem, upon still another humble subject. This additional calamity unnerves them, and they fall into each other's arms, sobbing poetically. They read together in silence, as follows:*

THE EARTHQUAKE-PRAYER.

'Twas a night of dread in Charleston, and the air was thick with fear;
Never yet had such a terror dropped its raven mantle here;
Never yet had deathly sorrow had so strange and sudden birth,
As upon the visitation of this tempest of the earth.

For the startled ground was surging as the waves of stormy seas,
And the belfries of the churches fell like stricken forest-trees;
And the walls that long had lorded over seen and unseen foe,
Covered thick with costly ruins this tornado from below!

---

* The manuscripts.

There were some who prayed God's presence who to God had long
    been near;
There were some for help entreating with repentance made of fear;
There were some who raved in madness through the long and mur-
    derous night;
There were corses calmly waiting for a mourner's tearful sight.

And that dark race whose religion has a superstitious trend,
But whose superstition clambers toward an everlasting Friend,
They were shouting in their frenzy, or in terror meekly dumb;
For they thought the opening signal of the Judgment Day had
    come.

But there sudden rose among them one of earth's untutored kings,
One of those unlooked-for leaders whom an hour of danger brings;
And he prayed—as souls do often, full of sympathy and love—
Partly to the souls around him, partly to the God above.

And he said: "I guess it's come, Lawd—dis yer day we've prayed so
    long—
For de symptoms all aroun' here dey be mos' tremendous strong;
But we ain't quite ready yet, Lawd, neber min' how well prepared,
We feel safe in Thy good mercy, but we're ebberlastin' scared!

"For You see we're mos'ly human when de grave comes re'lly
    nigh,
An' de spirit wants its freedom, but de flesh it hates to die!
We've been teasin' You for hebben all de summer long, I know;
But we ain't in half de hurry dat we was a while ago.

"When we come to look de facts through, in de light ob pain an' fear,
Dere is holes in all our armor dat at first view didn't appear;
An' we'd like to patch 'em over, if it's all de same to You;
Put it off a yeah, for certain—or perhaps You'd make it two!

"Then we've got some poor relations who may neber see Thy face
If dey do not earn de riches ob de sin-destroyin' grace;
Lawd, protect dem wid Thy patience, jus' de same-like as before,
An' keep diggin' roun' dose fig-trees for anudder year or more!

"BUT THERE SUDDEN ROSE AMONG THEM ONE OF EARTH'S UNTUTORED KINGS."

Fifth Chain.   133

"Let 'em off a little longer! In de light ob dis event,
Dey may recognize de season as a fine one to repent!
Dey will like Ye when dey know Ye, an' be glad to enter in,
An' dere's some dat's awful good, Lawd, ef it wasn't for deir sin!

"Dis yer world has lots of fine folks, who is anxious, I'm afraid,
For to pick a little longer 'fore dey have deir baskets weighed;
An' dere'd be a large major'ty who would vote, it must be owned,
For to hab de world's big fun'ral eberlastin'ly pos'poned!

"An' You know, O good deah Fathah, dat Your time is all home-
    made,
An' a thousan' years is nothin' in your golden steel-yards weighed;
Keep de same ol' footstool yet, Lawd; hol' it steady, I implore!
It'll maybe suit You better if You use it jes once more!

"But ob co'se our weak-eyed wisdom's like a rain-drop in de sea,
An' we ain't got any business to be mendin' plans for Thee;
If it's time to leave dese quarters an' go somewhar else to board,
Make de journey jes as easy as Your justice can afford!

"An' we know You hab a fondness for de average human soul,
So we'll hab consid'ble courage at de callin' ob de roll;
You're our sure 'nuff livin' Fathah—You're our fathahs' God an'
    frien'—
To de Lawd be praise an' glory, now an' evermore! Amen!"

'Twas a day of peace in Charleston, after many days of dread,
And the shelterless were sheltered, and the hungry had been fed;
And the death-invaded city through its misery now could grope,
And look forward to a future fringed with happiness and hope.

And those faithful dusky Christians will maintain for evermore,
That the fervent prayers they offered drove destruction from their
    shore;
And how much faith moves a mountain, or commands a rock to stay,
Is unknown to earthly ignorance, and for only God to say.

9*

SIXTH CHAIN.

Sixth Chain.

SCENE I., *suburbs of the city of Quebec, in the early morning of December 31, 1775. The air is full of falling snow. Wind whirls the flakes drearily, and piles them into drifts. A band of American soldiers are waiting to storm a barrier thrown across the street. They have sustained a heroic march through the forests and mountain passes of Maine and Canada, to make this fight. Colonel Benedict Arnold, their leader, addresses them.*

BENEDICT ARNOLD.[*]
Men of the Western world, you stand before
The mighty throne of England; that pursues
Its conquests o'er the heights of ocean hills,
And through the depths of your own forest waves;
That offers peace, if you will but accept
Handcuffs and shackles with it; that perhaps
May let you live within your wilderness,
If you will crouch in cabins of disgrace,
And feed their foreign lordships. You have come
Through all the dangers Nature could invent,
Through all the suffering cruelty could ask,
And fought, meanwhile, a constant, marching war,
With rocks and hills—with forests and with floods;
But all that you thus far have done, has been
The sowing of a seed, whose harvest now
Stands nodding just before you. Will you reap
This field of glory?
    VOICES (*with a hoarse cheer*).
                   We will follow you
Through death, and anything that lies beyond!

---

[*] The three legends of this chain endeavor to exhibit, in dramatic form, the probable thoughts and feelings of one of the most remarkable characters of history--under three widely differing sets of circumstances.

ARNOLD.
Riches await you if you win this fight,
Honor awaits you if you win this fight,
Glory awaits you if you win this fight—
    SOLDIER (*aside, shivering as he grasps his snow-covered musket*).
I did not leave my well-loved forest home,
I did not leave my wife and mother weeping,
I did not leave my blue-eyed baby sleeping,
Through these vast forest solitudes to roam,
For honor or for glory or for gold.
In three great words my motto can be told:
God, Liberty, and Right!
                      For these I fight.
    ARNOLD (*continuing*).
Now let me say a word to any one
Not friendly to this contest: if one's here
Whose craven heart is still as yet untuned
To the wild concert-pitch of war, I say
Get out! go back! no bridges have been burned;
Safe hospitals and beds upon the way
Will take your puny, worthless bodies in.
I shall be at the front! I can not stay
Behind, to spur a coward to his duty.
Go back—weak woman by all women scorned!
But if there be those here who do not know
What life means, without glory; those whose hearts
Find mountain air, even, poisoned, when it floats
Above a land disgraced, come on with me!
And if you live, the world shall crown you heroes;
And if you die, though we've no Westminster
Where you can be entombed in marble, yet
Your names will bivouac in the nation's heart.
    Hoarse VOICES.
Give us the word to charge!
    ARNOLD.   Now charge, and conquer!

    [*They fight their way fiercely through the first barrier;* ARNOLD *is wounded and disabled, and led to the rear, his soldiers still fighting.*

"... WILL YOU REAP THIS FIELD OF GLORY?"

Sixth Chain. 141

ARNOLD (*as he is carried bleeding past his soldiers*).
Fight on, my men, for glory—riches—fame!
 SOLDIER (*grasping more tightly his musket*).
God, Liberty, and Right—direct *my* aim!

SCENE II., *the city of Philadelphia. A room in* ARNOLD'S *headquarters. Time, January,* 1780. *He holds in his hand a written reprimand from General Washington, which a court-martial had ordered administered. He paces the floor like a caged panther.*

ARNOLD.
I have decided!—Let these ragged men,
These poverty-accoutred colonists
Playing "Republic" at a dime a day,
Shirk for themselves—stripped of their strongest hope!
This hacked-up sword, that I so oft have worn
In a red sheath of blood—blood of their foes—
And been abused for all my pains and pain,
Shall join the cast-off cutlery of fools,
  [*Throwing it, crashing, to the floor.*
And I will take the bright, gold-hilted blade,
Flashing with gems, that England offers me—
Then hew and stab my way to wealth and power.
A nation fights for self—why not a man?
Man *is* a nation! with rich provinces
Of heart and soul and brain; and his success
Is more to him than other men's to him!

They'll say, "He is a traitor." Let them howl!
Has not Dame Nature given me the cue?
The head-wind is a traitor to the sail;
The tempest is a traitor to the ship;
The white frost is a traitor to the vine;
The conflagration traitor to the house—
And all were friends—until good reasons changed
Their love to venom. And have I not cause
To shift my blood-drenched loyalty about?
What has this puling "nation," with thirteen
Unluckily numbered colonies, e'er done

To pay me for myself?—What has it given?
Honor?—What flags has this frail sinking craft
With which to cover even a chieftain's corpse?
My epaulettes are rags; my titles scorned
By the same foe that I so oft have driven.
The English call *him* "Mr. Washington,"
And me plain Arnold. Honor!—a good joke!
So, what have these wild upstarts given me,
To pay me for myself? Is't money?—Well,
When brass breeds gold, and lead yields diamonds,
And promises are dollars, then my pay
Will be a general's meed, and not a serf's!

What has this Congress given to me? One who
Had suffered fifty deaths that they might live—
Had climbed and swam from Boston to Quebec—
Had conquered cataracts, and frosts, and cliffs,
Then fallen—wounded almost to the death—
Fighting for them?—what dulcet word of cheer
Has Congress offered me to heal my wounds?
"Spendthrift, come here and settle your accounts!"
When I on Lake Champlain stood by my ship
'Mid smoking, crackling masts, and sails, and spars—
And still fought with the foe—fought them from hell!—
What did they do to pay me for my blood?
Promoted men above me, who had yet
To learn the smell of powder! When beneath
My fallen steed a duel I had waged
With the foe's army—what magnificent gift
Did Congress tender me?—Another horse!
As if to say, "If you will ride to death
In our supreme behalf, we'll pay your fare." . . .
The card is played!—I am a British subject!—

    A Voice *seems to speak to him:*
Arnold, beware!—A traitor's name
   Is heavy to be borne;
Drag not your life through sloughs of shame—
   Seek not a nation's scorn!

Sixth Chain.

He who betrays his land of birth,
Beckons for hell while yet on earth.

Arnold, step back!—You stand before
  The coming century's tread!
Men yet to live may curse you sore,
  Long after you are dead!
The brave man treacherous to the brave,
Must suffer, even in the grave.

 ARNOLD (*fiercely, grasping his sword from the floor*).
Whose voice is that? Coward, come out and fight!
Clash not dull words with me; but try your sword.
Who are you?   [*An interval of silence.*
   No one's here. . . . It was my fancy.
I am alone. Yet Solitude to-day
Is grievous company. I'll call my servant,
And test him slyly if he'll go with me.   [*Rings.*

   Enter MIKE, *a servant.*
ARNOLD.
Mike, this is quite a long and weary war.
 MIKE.
 Yes, sirrh, but bedad it'll be longher and strongher and higher and lower and deeper and bloodier—before we ever give up!
 Bedad, before we'll ever give up—we'll foight 'em till we can foight no more—and aftherwards, too—a long time aftherwards, bedad.
 ARNOLD.
Mike, there are those who think we best had yield.
 MIKE.
 YALDE?—GIVE UP?—SURRENDHER? Sure, sirrh, that will never happen until the hottest place known in sachred or profane histhory frazes over; and then, bedad, we'll put on the skates and have at 'em!
 Gineral, I have two little bize—one of them a girrul; sure this same little girrul, she is growin' up to be her mother, right over and over again, widout her infirmities of temper.
 Gineral, I like that little girrul pretty well; sure she is the only crature in the wurruld that ever set me to writhin' po'try! and I sind

her poems ivery day that no one but hersilf can undherstand, and she not ould enough;

I fell in love wid her the very day she was born, and me love—it has incr'ased daily since.

But, Gineral, sooner than I would see our little Republic surrendher, I would take that little girrul, kiss her good-by, and lay her away in her coffin forever. [*Exit.*

ARNOLD.

Good heavens! how drear and lonely 'tis, even now,
This turning on one's Country! but 'tis done;
The card is played; I am a British subject!

SCENE III., *a hotel room near the city of London in* 1794—*twelve years after the close of the Revolutionary War. An American sits alone at a table writing. A card is handed him by a servant.*

AMERICAN.
Ah, Talleyrand!—what can he want with me?
Send him up.
Enter TALLEYRAND.
   Pardon, Monsieur Anderson?
 AMERICAN (*rising*).
General, sir.
 TALLEYRAND.
   Pardon. Parlez vous Français?
 AMERICAN.
Not well.
 TALLEYRAND.
   Then let us in the English talk,
Which I know little of, but still can use.
I beg you, General, listen now to me.
I have been worked much for my country. I
Have toiled and suffered hard; it gives me naught
Except allow me still much more to toil.
It says to me: "We do not want you, now;"
England replies, "We do not want you here."
And so my heart—true to my country's weal,

Sixth Chain.

I carry to your land of liberty,
Hoping my fortune may be nurtured there,
Till it and I rush to my country's aid.
Meanwhile, I ask you, General, that you give
Me letters to some friends in yonder land—
    AMERICAN (*rising eagerly to his feet*).
What, friends?—You say I've friends out there?—Speak quick.
Who are they?—Let me know their names!—Speak quick!
You shall have letters.—Speak!
    TALLEYRAND (*shrugging his shoulders*).
                            Why, General,
I know not who *your* friends may be; I know
Who *mine* are; they are those I love right well—
Those that are true to me, and I to them;
I hope some time my country all will say,
"Talleyrand was our friend." Not now, but some time!
You surely have friends in your fatherland?
Send me to even the humblest!
    AMERICAN.
                         Talleyrand,
If you should pace my country, east to west,
And north to south, and cry out as you walked,
"Where are the friends of this man?—A reward
I offer to whome'er to me will bring
A friend of him whose name this letter bears!"
Then you would cry to all that Western land
In vain.—Yet not through silence would you walk:
Curses would leap at you from every door;
Hate's maledictions pierce you through and through;
Scorn would creep round you with its withering hiss;
Only because you named me as a friend.
Women and men and children all would cry,
"Curse him forever!"
    TALLEYRAND.
                   General, why is that?
Were you not brave?
    AMERICAN (*laughing*).
                   BRAVE? ask them was I not?
Ask any one that e'er crossed swords with me,

Was I not brave? Ask you of any one,
Peer or subaltern, where was I i' the fight?
Did I say "Go," or "Come!" Brave?—Try me now!
I was th' Achilles of the western fields!
Had I been marshalled in the Trojan wars,
Homer my praises would be singing yet!
I would be still a king 'mongst western kings—
Had I been true—
 TALLEYRAND.
     True?
 AMERICAN.
       Talleyrand, list to me.
You speak of friends: you have true friends on earth—
You have some good friends in th' Elysian fields:
They have marched on, and camp there till you come.
Hearts you have tied to; souls that reach for yours;
You know not, happy man, what 'tis to be
Without one friend, in all God's threefold realm!
 TALLEYRAND.
Without one friend?
 AMERICAN.
      I speak it with my heart!
I have no friend in earth, or heaven, or hell!
If I were brought before the bar of God,
For final judgment, and it should be said,
"If there be any one in all this throng
Can speak one word for him, he shall be saved,"
All would be still, in thorny, scornful silence,
And I be pushed down, headlong, to my doom.
Worse than my doom; for Satan would appear
At his white-heated iron gate, and shout
"You are too vile to come as others do—
Too treacherous—you would give away the pass!
Delve midst the sulphurous filth outside, and then
Sneak upward from beneath!"
 TALLEYRAND (*aside*).
      Insane!—insane!
 AMERICAN (*overhearing*).
No! no! too sane! too sane! would I might rave!

"I HAVE NO FRIEND IN EARTH, OR HEAVEN, OR HELL!"

Sixth Chain.

I would pay well for lunacy's drum-roll
To drown the clamor of my thoughts! Too sane!
God gave to me clear brain—metallic will—
Warm heart—credentials of a prince 'mongst men;
But after me that hell-spawned spirit came—
The partner of all traitor-craft; the one
That helped foul Judas count his silver coins,
And changed them into lead to sink his soul;
That crept up even to Satan ere he fell,
And whispered, "You can rule instead of God!"
   TALLEYRAND.
For God's sake, man, who are you?—what your crime?
   AMERICAN.
'Tis hell enough, to think this day by day;
But when night comes—the horror-breeding night—
The black page where are written lurid things
We will not see or hear by day—there throng
In the dull currents of my sleep—fierce souls,
Swarming from dread, cold silences of death.
One word they whisper in my aching ears,
Till it becomes a shout! It walks my brain,
And leaves its tracks in branded letters there;
Oh, I can look within, and read it now!
Midnight court-martial they hold over me—
They try me o'er and o'er for the same crime;
No one is there to speak a word for me;
And the same verdict always follows—"GUILTY!"
And the same sentence—"DO NOT LET HIM DIE!"
   TALLEYRAND.
Tell me your crime, man, tell me!
   AMERICAN.
                          Talleyrand,
You yet are young; you have the columns still
Perchance, of swiftly marching years to form.
Take this advice from an old worn-out man—
Worn from without—worn threadbare from within;
Be never false to man; it is a crime;
But if you are, man some time may forget it;
Be never false to woman; 'tis a crime

Greater; but woman, heaven-like, may forgive.
Be never false to childhood; 'tis a crime
Worst of all three; perhaps God may forgive.
But ne'er betray your country, till you wish
To pull the red-hot roof of hell upon you!
  Talleyrand.
What did you do?
  American.
       I'll tell you; nearer! nearer!
Let me not speak, but whisper the damned truth!
I took my country's honor from her eyes,
I took my country's favors from her hand,
I took my country's strongest-guarded hope,
Her fortress, heaven-walled by river and hill,
Key to her hopes—hope of the centuries—
I took all these—intrusted me by her—
Took them in my black hands on one black night,
And—sold them—sold them—sold them—sold them—sold them
As I would vend a paltry patch of earth,
As I would huckster off a senseless beast—
Sold them for some few paltry chips of gold—
Of rotting, rotten, senseless, beastly gold!
I sold the Western Hemisphere, and then,
Poor fool, could not deliver the goods!
  Talleyrand (*rising*).
           Your name!
  American.
Listen! while I repeat to you the name
Of one once grandest of the grand, now base—
So low and vile that men would not even use it
To step upon, to keep them from the mud!
Benedict Arnold, traitor!

SEVENTH CHAIN.

Seventh Chain.

SCENE, *the cozy back parlor of a city residence. An old-fashioned grandmother is sitting in the most pleasant corner, with knitting-work on her lap. A lady teacher from some neighboring boarding-school sits near by, with a book in her hand. Subdued strains of music come from the front parlor, where* KATHERINE, *the good old lady's favorite granddaughter, is practising a brilliant overture.*

GRANDMOTHER.

I'm glad that it suited you, School-ma'am, to spend a few days here
    with Kate:
You're both of you fine-wove and crisp-like, an' take to each other
    first-rate.
When woman-hearts tangle together, they twist round again and again,
An' make up a queer sort o' love-match I never have noticed in
    men.
And, School-ma'am, I'm thriftily anxious about this smart gran'child
    o' mine,
An' want to talk candid about her, with present an' future design.

She's hungry for other folks' knowledge, an' never too full to be
    fed;
She's packed every book that I know of, all open-leaved, like, in her
    head;
The 'rithmetic makes its home with her; the grammar is proud of
    her tongue;
She spells words as if she had made 'em, 'way back when the lan-
    guage was young.
She knows all the g'ography found yet; she'd feel in a manner at
    home,
If dropped in the streets of J'rus'lem, or woke up some mornin' in
    Rome.

She's studied the habits of planets—knows how to call names at a star—
She's traced their invisible railroads, an' tells what their time-tables are;
She's learnin' the language of heathens, that good-minded people abhorred—
A-thwartin' the old Tower of Babel—undoin' the work of the Lord.
Yes, Teacher, our dear, pretty Kath'rine is very sleek-minded an' smart;
But still I can't help but to worry concernin' the breadth o' her heart!

Teacher.

Why! sympathies need not to narrow, because the brain clambers above;
The more that a genuine heart knows, the better it knows how to love.
A gem was all crowded with splendor, unseen in the gloom of the mines:
'Tis not now the less of a diamond because it is polished, and shines!
The flower that was hunted by wild weeds, thinks never to blossom less fair,
Because it is borne to a garden, and tended with wisdom and care.
A lamp in the sky had been tarnished by cloud-birds that flew from afar;
The wind swept the mist from its brightness—it gleamed, all the more of a star!
Whate'er is at fault in your grandchild, her learning makes easier withstood;
Whatever is good in your grandchild, her learning makes only more good.

Grandmother.

That's nice, soothin' sentiments, School-ma'am, an' helps all that works in your line;
It's one o' your golden opinions—I wish that it also was mine!
But, Teacher, suppose that she marries:—the knives of her brain bright an' keen—
An' knows all creation, excep' how to keep her house cozy and clean!

Suppose when her husband comes home tired, the cheer o' her table to seek,
She feeds him with steak that is soggy, an' tells him its meanin' in Greek?
Suppose that her coffee is muddy as if it was dipped from a trench:
Will that make his stomach less homesick, because she can tell it in French?
Suppose that her help is her master, along o' the things she don't know:
Can algebra make up the diff'rence, or grammar-books give her a show?
Oh, School-ma'am, those women keep house best (with nothin' to say ag'in *you*)
Who've learned to keep house o' their mothers, an' worked all its alphabet through!

TEACHER.
Your grandchild must choose for her husband, a man with an intellect wide,
Who makes of the well-guarded body a place for the soul to reside;
Whose home is a God-made cathedral, with heart-blessings clear-voiced and sweet;
Who comes back at night for soul-comfort—not simply for what he can eat.
Who thinks with her, feels with her, helps her—has patience, for both of their sakes;
Who celebrates all her successes, and takes stock in all her mistakes.
Who treasures her well-taught advantage o'er one who unstudied begins;
Who welcomes with sweet-whispered pleasure each step of the race that she wins.
Who leads her to minds that are kindled with brands from the watch-fires of fame;
Who's glad that her lamp has been trimmed well, to catch the clear sanctified flame.

GRANDMOTHER.
An' if she shouldn't find this cur'os'ty?

TEACHER.   Then let her as single be known;
And thank God her training has taught her to work out life's problem alone!

Grandmother.

But, School-ma'am, admittin' your arg'ment (if one can "admit" what one don't),
We'll say that she'll marry an angel (though likelier 'twill happen she won't);
But s'posin' she does, an' her children are sent, same as others, to school:
I worry 'bout whether she'll let 'em be taught by the brain-stuffin' rule.
It hurts me to see 'em build over a child into somebody's "pride,"
Through givin' him heartaches each week-day, by poundin' his head from inside!
They make 'em bite books with their teethin'; grown studies run all through their play;
They're killin' the children by inches, with five or six studies a day.
They load 'em with large definitions—as big as the children are small;
Ah me! it's a wonder the poor things twist up into grown folks at all!
There's many a poor little cre'tur' with other folks' words over-filled,
Not only "made mad" by "much learning" but weakened an' sickened an' killed!
There's many a green little grass-mound, whose tenant would say, could it talk,
"I died by their tryin' to run me, before I was able to walk!"

Teacher.

A blessing's no less of a blessing, because by some one 'tis abused;
The air, fire, and water *can* murder—and yet they all have to be used.
The steed that we drive to the river, is tempted, not tortured, to drink;
The child should be given thought-burdens—but only to teach him to think.
Take comfort from now for the future; for Katherine, with all that she knows,
Is bright as a dollar just minted, and fresh as a new-blossomed rose.

Grandmother.

But, School-ma'am, I worry (you notice I'm built in a worryin' way,
And ne'er will learn how not to worry, clean up to my uttermost day)
'Bout whether my granddaughter Kath'rine will nourish her children to home,
Or let them run loose, so she sweetly through charity's pleasures can roam?

"THERE'S MANY A GREEN LITTLE GRASS-MOUND."

Seventh Chain. 159

I worried my children up safely—I care for my grandchildren too—
I want my great-grandchildren cared for—so *their* children also will do.
Just read how three poor little creatur's, who—born too luxurious and high
To reach happy home and its comforts—were left by their mother to die!

TEACHER *reads from a scrap-book:*

KIDNAPPED IN MERCY.

I.

Through long, bright paths of The Gold Streeted Town,
Three angels walked, one day, to make a tour
In the rude country districts of wide space.
They sped past mansions built of costly gems—
Past steeples, minarets, and spires of gold;
They crossed a coral bridge on silver wires,
Swinging above a clear-voiced stream; they walked
Through parks that in their laps held sweet bouquets,
And in their hands waved grand, immortal trees;
They passed through all heart-splendors realized—
Through every pure dream of their lives—come true!

Now, ere they stepped out into cold, wide space,
And turned the cloud-like hill that hid The Town,
They trained their eyes on the magnificence
Of the half-distant city, as if going
For many years—instead of one short day.

Along the dusty turnpikes of cold space,
These angels walked; they crossed wide avenues
That led to stars of various size and tint.
One there was, where a gilded finger-post
Said, "To the planet Venus." There was one
That read, "This way to Neptune."—All the stars
Were listed in the guideposts that they saw.

And yet they turned not, right nor left; although
Their passports, sealed in Heaven, would shelter them

Where'er they willed to go; they could have known
Where queenly Saturn found her diamond rings;
How the striped juggler, Jupiter, can toss
Four worlds as playthings round his stalwart form;
They could have seen th' attendants of the sun
Feed full each hour his hot electric fires;

They passed all these, and came to a small lane,
Barred by a gate, sagging on one weak hinge,
With slats part stained and rusted o'er with blood,
But now and then a wire of pure bright gold;
Whose latch was set with bright bewildering gems,
One view of which built passion's wildest fire;
But with sharp, gleaming knives concealed within,
That cut the hand that lifted up the latch.
This was a road to Earth; and here they paused,
Raised the bright, treacherous bolt, and entered through.
Earth once had been their own sweet, bitter home,
And still they sadly loved to visit here.

Through flowers almost as sweet as Heaven could grow,
Through loathsome, bad-faced weeds that bit and stung,
Past silver-throated birds that made the trees,
Even, seem to sing—o'er serpents coiled and fierce—
Past wild brutes that would tear the world in two,
And white, sweet lambs that loved their angel guests,
And journeyed after them, and kissed their hands—
Down this long, crookèd, sharp-contrasted lane,
These angels walked: they were upon The Earth.

No scenery here, but was each hour surpassed
In their new home; no architecture grand,
More than a feeble parody on Heaven.
What walked they here to see?—They came to help.

In a rough city road, they met with three
Small children, wandering desolate about,
Searching for something that would feed their minds,
And please their fancies; searching wistfully,

"HE STAYS AT OUR HOUSE NIGHTS."

Seventh Chain.

And weariedly, and with sad countenance,
For something that would cheer their desolate hearts.

One was a tiny warrior: he had fought
With coarser urchins, till his chubby face
Was scratched and bruised;—one was a pretty girl,
Who made herself believe that rows of stones
Were mansion walls; she had her little rooms,
Each with the sky for ceiling. In one nook,
She kept a homely, patched-up doll, and oft
Above it crooned, and kissed it with love-looks.
Another little girl, with dark, weird eyes,
Was gazing at the clouds, as if she longed
To fly with them. But all looked desolate;
And near to them, three loathsome shadow-fiends
Laughed with each other—at the children leered—
And whispered, "They are certain to be ours."

By toil, and pain, and many a prayer to God,
The angels dressed themselves in mortal shape,
And kindly called the children.—They all came,
With tears of pleasure framed in eager eyes,
And hunger in their hearts. 'Twas many a day
Since they had had such restful, loving words.

"Where is your mother, little one?" was asked.
"Oh, she is at a grand reception, ma'am."
"Where was she yesterday?" "At some great feast,
With many other ladies."—"Day before?"
"Out at the Home for Helpless Children, ma'am."
"When does she let you see her?"—"Only just
Once in a while. But Nurse is good to us,
And goes and visits with another nurse,
And lets us run about, and play alone."

"Where is your father, little ones?" was said.
"Why, Papa?—let me see;—we have one yet—
He lives in town, but stays at our house nights.
I saw him, only just a month ago.

He's very large and pretty—but—he scowls.
He's getting rich, or something of that kind."

And still the shadow-fiends together laughed,
And whispered to each other, "They are ours."

II.

Once more through paths of The Gold Streeted Town,
These angels walked; and at Heaven's outer gate,
Another angel joined them—dressed in black.

Far in the country districts of wide space,
Again they journeyed.—When, this time, was reached
The gate of Earth—Night stood there, dark and cold.

Through the long, winding lane they walked; and then,
On silent streets, by Earth's great shadow hushed.

Through thrice-locked doors, up lofty velvet stairs
Of a great mansion, crept the silent four.
Three children lay upon luxurious cots,
Restlessly sleeping;—one, with tear-stained face,
Mourned the lost, threadbare doll she loved so well;
Another curved his brow and shook his fist
Against some foe he had in Dream-land met;
The third lay sleeping, with a pretty smile,
Half hoping and half sure her dreams were true;
But all looked piteous, sad, and desolate.
And over them the loathsome shadow-fiends
Laughed with each other—at the children leered—
And whispered, "They are certain to be ours."

Softly the angel clothed in black, bent down,
And kissed the little sleepers; a slight pang
Vexed each pale face, and then three forms emerged
From the frail bodies, looking like to them,
But purer far, and sweeter. With a smile,
They gazed up at the looks of love they saw,

And trembling with the first pure heart-delight
They ever yet had known, soft kissed the lips
That bent to them and whispered, "Come with us."
And then they walked to The Gold Streeted Town.

Then Faith, one of the angels, said, "Right true
We were to these sweet colonists of ours;
And it has been as God said it must be."
And Hope replied, "The lives we have just saved,
Will learn to help and pity other lives."
And Charity—chief of the three—exclaimed,
"Poor parents! when they find their little ones
Sleeping so cold, with Death's thin covering,
They will remember all the sad neglect
Their careless selfishness around them threw,
And some time will be richer for their loss."

And Death said, "Farewell; I can only go
Far as the gates; I ne'er can enter in;
I do God's work, but never see His home;"
And wrapped his black cloak round him, and was gone.

GRANDMOTHER.

Now s'p'osin' that Kath'rine should turn out a mother like that one, some day,
An' let my great-gran'childr'n suffer till Heaven had to take 'em away?
Suppose, that in holdin' together outside homes that pull at her heart,
She lets her own fam'ly run helpless, an' sees her own home fall apart?
She's al'ays herself sacrificin' for others; which, when people do,
They'll sacrifice, if they ain't careful, the ones that is nearest 'em too.

TEACHER.

If love and not pride is the reason our good deeds about us are strown,
They help us be true to our loved ones—they make us more fond of our own.

If Charity feeds on Heaven's goodness, and not on Earth's senseless
    display,
'Twill care first for those who are nearest, and lead them the same
    lofty way.
True charity comes from the heart-depths, and not from pride's glit-
    tering foam;
Remember—"the light that shines farthest, shines always the bright-
    est at home!"

    GRANDMOTHER.

But, Teacher, I worry 'cause Kath'rine—of nothin' partic'l'r afraid—
Gets humbugged, annoyed, an'·imposed on, by those she is tryin' to aid;
The folks that she lends, never pay her; the gratitude does not come
    roun';
I b'lieve that that girl has been humbugged by half of the beggars
    in town!

    TEACHER.

Life throngs with experiments; most things we do, are the planting
    of grain:
Perhaps we are building gold harvests—perchance we may fruitless
    remain.
On ruins of many a century the edifice stands as we gaze;
A splendid success, loved of Heaven, full many a failure repays.
    [*Turns a few leaves of the scrap-book, and reads:*

LADY BOUNTIFUL'S TRIUMPH.

She was modestly winsome, and stylishly fair,
And the sunbeams had spun the rich skeins of her hair,
And her eyes were as bright as pure diamonds be,
And her form had the grace of a zephyr-tossed tree;
She was "pretty," some whispered, and "handsome," some said,
And "beautiful" others described her instead;
And covetous glances were after her sent,
And flattery followed wherever she went.

And her heart was as soft as her ribbons were gay,
And she loved all the world, in a general way

(For the hard jailer Fashion, with all of his art,
Can not chain up a really generous heart),
And her white hand was open, to prince or to boor,
If he only was ragged, and wretched, and poor.

And her husband coined lucre from day unto day,
And she faithfully struggled to give it away;
For if he from the world to win gold had a knack,
She esteemed it her part to pay some of it back!
And Charity knows very well how it thrives,
When 'tis zealously managed by rich people's wives;
There's many a lady, whose alms would ill fare,
If it wasn't for a selfish old husband somewhere!

And he smiled on her giving (she gave, as he knew,
A dollar, where he made a thousand or two);
But his smile had the feel of a good-natured sneer;
For *he* fought with the world, and approached it more near;
And he noticed that all is not Want that complains,
And that Charity often is scorned for its pains;
That the unctuous asking of alms is a gift,
And that Poverty, sometimes, itself, is a thrift;
And that he who will carelessly bounties accord,
Oft is lending to Satan, instead of the Lord.

And the first piteous mortal she happened to meet,
Was a woe-begone beggar, who crept thro' the street;
With face properly sad and form carefully bent,
And a mien that strewed sorrow wherever he went.
And she wondered what terrible lot could be worse,
And gave him such cash as she had in her purse;
And then went home at once, with a face like the sun,
With her' husband to share the good deed she had done.
But he laughingly said, when she pictured her friend,
"That poor scamp has a bank-book, and money to lend."
And she wept with vexation; and vowed not to give
To a beggar again, long as Heaven let her live.

And a little while after, it chanced to befall,
That a sad-looking gentleman made her a call;

With late news from her pastor; which bade her extend
To this brother afflicted, the hand of a friend.
And the sad-looking man drew a picture of gloom
Of a sick, wretched wife, in a comfortless room;
Of the bad luck around him accustomed to lurk,
And the way he had worked, that he might obtain work;
And he made her believe, that if help were not found,
He would starve, ere another bright Sabbath came round.
Then he offered for sale—sadly resolute still—
A small one-dollar book for a ten-dollar bill.
And sweet sympathy warmed up her heart, through and through,
And instead of one book, she invested in two;
And she waited her husband's home-coming, to run
And share with his heart the good deed she had done.
But the afternoon paper contained a hot sketch
Of this scamp, whom it called "an unprincipled wretch,"
Informing an oft-told community how
He had swindled for months, and was swindling them now;
And it gave a long history, gloomy with fact,
And a full-length description, absurdly exact.
So her husband she met with a pain-chastened grace,
And a queer look of innocent shame in her face;
And instead of her setting his heart all astir,
He employed the whole evening in comforting her.
And she vowed, if she lived to be ninety years old,
Of no agent again would she buy, and be sold.

And the next case of pity her heart chanced to greet,
Was a hand-organ woman who sat in the street;
Who, old and unfeminine, said not a word,
And played a queer tune that could scarcely be heard.
And 'twas plainly apparent, and hard not to see,
There were two wooden stumps where her feet ought to be.
And our sweet Lady Bountiful's heart nestled near
This sister, so palpably wretched and drear;
And she gave her enough, moved by Charity's call,
To buy the dame out—legs, hand-organ, and all.
And she went home at night with her heart all aglow
With the help she had given to this daughter of woe;

And this sweet-bread of deeds,—like a generous child
She shared with her best friend—who praised her, and smiled;
For he knew all the time, and so, shortly, did she,
That this pauper of streets was as rich as need be;
And had married a daughter, with splendor quite rare,
And had given to her jewels a duchess could wear.
And our dear Lady Bountiful drooped with dismay,
At having been tricked in this high-handed way,
And vowed none again with her bounty to greet,
Unless blessed with the requisite number of feet.

And the next, and the next, and the next, and the next
Of the times she was tricked, made her almost as vexed;
But there came, one dark evening, a gleam of surprise,
From a woman whose heart had a home in her eyes;
Whose words sweetly warmed her fair friend; for they burned
With gratitude true, that had truly been earned.
And she murmured, "To me you are dearer than breath;
You snatched me from sorrow, and suffering, and death;
You lifted a burden my soul could not bear;
You tided me over the rocks of despair.
You saved me my daughter—my husband—my son;
God bless you and yours, for the deeds you have done!"

And the lady's tired heart on this gratitude fed,
For her husband had happened to hear what was said;
And the man of the world—as a tear graced his eye—
Felt as if he had news from the world in the sky;
And he said to his wife, as her gemmed hand he pressed,
"This transaction defrays the expense of the rest."

GRANDMOTHER.
But, Teacher, I'll tell my main trouble (though less than the ones I have said);
I'm gettin' behind the times daily, while Kate keeps a-gettin' ahead.
She'll grow a fine lady, and nothin' between us in common there'll be;
Now don't you think, some time or other, that Kate'll be 'shamed, like, of me?

KATE (*entering and kissing* GRANDMOTHER).
Ashamed of you? Never!—I'd give more for one silver hair of your head,
Than all of the studies I know of, and all of the authors I've read!
Do you know, you absurd dear old grandma', your heart and your brain are more aid,
Than all of the sciences heard of, and all of the books ever made!
No process that man has discovered, will act out affection's pure part;
The brain of the head is a failure, compared to the brain of the heart!
Ashamed of you? Let your grand life-work an answer unqualified be!
Pray God that my life may be lived so you'll never be "'shamed like" of me!

THE END.

SELECTED HOME READING.

CARLETON'S POETICAL WORKS.
Illustrated. Square 8vo, Ornamental Cloth, $2 00; Gilt Edges, $2 50; Full Seal, $4 00.
CITY LEGENDS. By WILL CARLETON.
CITY BALLADS. By WILL CARLETON.
FARM FESTIVALS. By WILL CARLETON.
FARM LEGENDS. By WILL CARLETON.
FARM BALLADS. By WILL CARLETON.

HARPER'S CYCLOPÆDIA OF BRITISH AND AMERICAN POETRY.
Harper's Cyclopædia of British and American Poetry. Edited by EPES SARGENT. Large 8vo, Illuminated Cloth, Colored Edges, $4 50.

POETS OF THE NINETEENTH CENTURY.
Poets of the Nineteenth Century. Selected and Edited by the Rev. ROBERT ARIS WILLMOTT. With English and American Additions, arranged by EVERT A. DUYCKINCK. New and Enlarged Edition. Superbly illustrated with 141 engravings. In elegant small 4to form, printed on Superfine Tinted Paper, richly bound in Extra Cloth, Bevelled, Gilt Edges, $5 00; Half Calf, $5 50; Full Turkey Morocco, $9 00.

THE POETS AND POETRY OF SCOTLAND.
The Poets and Poetry of Scotland. From the Earliest to the Present Time. Comprising Characteristic Selections from the Works of the more Noteworthy Scottish Poets, with Biographical and Critical Notices. By JAMES GRANT WILSON. With Portraits on Steel. 2 vols., 8vo, Cloth, $10 00; Cloth, Gilt Edges, $11 00; Half Calf, $14 50; Full Morocco, $18 00.

FRIENDLY EDITION OF SHAKESPEARE'S WORKS.
Friendly Edition of Shakespeare's Works. Edited by W. J. ROLFE. In 20 volumes. Illustrated. 16mo, Sheets, $27 00, Cloth, $30 00; Half Calf, $60 00. (*In a Box.*)

SHAKSPEARE'S DRAMATIC WORKS.
Shakspeare's Dramatic Works. The Dramatic Works of Shakspeare, with the Corrections and Illustrations of Dr. JOHNSON, G. STEEVENS, and others. Revised by ISAAC REED. Illustrated. 6 vols., Royal 12mo, Cloth, $9 00, Sheep, $11 40.

FOLK-LORE OF SHAKESPEARE.
Folk-Lore of Shakespeare. By the Rev. T. F. THISELTON DYER, M.A., Oxon. 8vo, Cloth, $2 50.

SHAKSPERE: A CRITICAL STUDY OF HIS MIND AND ART.
Shakspere: A Critical Study of his Mind and Art. By EDWARD DOWDEN, LL.D., Vice-President of "The New Shakspere Society." 12mo, Cloth, $1 75.

THE WORKS OF OLIVER GOLDSMITH.
The Works of Oliver Goldsmith. Edited by PETER CUNNINGHAM, F.S.A. From New Electrotype Plates. 4 vols., 8vo, Cloth, Paper Labels, Uncut Edges and Gilt Tops, $8 00, Sheep, $10 00; Half Calf, $17 00.

ROLFE'S ENGLISH CLASSICS.
Edited, with Notes, by W. J. ROLFE, A.M. Illustrated. Small 4to, Flexible Cloth, 56 cents per volume; Paper, 40 cents per volume.

SELECT POEMS OF GOLDSMITH.—SELECT POEMS OF THOMAS GRAY.—SELECT POEMS OF ROBERT BROWNING.—BROWNING'S DRAMAS.—MILTON'S MINOR POEMS.—MACAULAY'S LAYS OF ANCIENT ROME.—WORDSWORTH'S SELECT POEMS.

SHAKESPEARE'S THE TEMPEST.—MERCHANT OF VENICE.—KING HENRY THE EIGHTH.—JULIUS CÆSAR.—RICHARD THE SECOND.—MACBETH.—MIDSUMMER NIGHT'S DREAM.—KING HENRY THE FIFTH.—KING JOHN.—AS YOU LIKE IT.—KING HENRY IV. Part I.—KING HENRY IV. Part II.—HAMLET.—MUCH ADO ABOUT NOTHING.—ROMEO AND JULIET.—OTHELLO.—TWELFTH NIGHT.—THE WINTER'S TALE.—RICHARD THE THIRD.—KING LEAR.—ALL'S WELL THAT ENDS WELL.—CORIOLANUS.—TAMING OF THE SHREW.—CYMBELINE.—THE COMEDY OF ERRORS.—ANTONY AND CLEOPATRA.—MEASURE FOR MEASURE.—MERRY WIVES OF WINDSOR.—LOVE'S LABOUR'S LOST.—TIMON OF ATHENS.—TWO GENTLEMEN OF VERONA.—TROILUS AND CRESSIDA.—HENRY VI. Part I.—HENRY VI. Part II.—HENRY VI. Part III.—PERICLES, PRINCE OF TYRE.—THE TWO NOBLE KINSMEN.—VENUS AND ADONIS, &c.—SONNETS.—TITUS ANDRONICUS.

SWINTON'S STUDIES IN ENGLISH LITERATURE.
Studies in English Literature: being Typical Selections of British and American Authorship, from Shakespeare to the Present Time; together with Definitions, Notes, Analyses, and Glossary, as an aid to Systematic Literary Study. By Professor WILLIAM SWINTON, A.M., Author of "Harper's Language Series." With Portraits, Crown 8vo, Cloth, $1 50.

TENNYSON'S SONGS, WITH MUSIC.
Songs from the Published Writings of Alfred Tennyson. Set to Music by various Composers. Edited by W. G. CUSINS. With Portrait and Original Illustrations by Winslow Homer, C. S. Reinhart, A. Fredericks, and Jessie Curtis. Royal 4to, Cloth, Gilt Edges, $5 00.

TENNYSON'S WORKS.
Complete Works of Alfred, Lord Tennyson. Poet-Laureate. With an Introductory Sketch by ANNE THACKERAY RITCHIE. With Portraits and Illustrations. Pages 430. 8vo, Cloth, $2 00, Gilt Edges, $2 50.

BRUCE'S OLD HOMESTEAD POEMS.
Old Homestead Poems. By WALLACE BRUCE. Illustrated. Square 8vo, Cloth, $2 00.

THE BOOK OF GOLD, AND OTHER POEMS.
The Book of Gold, and Other Poems. By J. T. TROWBRIDGE. Ill'd. 8vo, Ornamental Covers, Gilt Edges $2 50.

HALPINE'S (MILES O'REILLY) POEMS.
Halpine's (Miles O'Reilly) Poems. With a Biographical Sketch and Explanatory Notes. Edited by ROBERT B. ROOSEVELT. Portrait on Steel. Post 8vo, Cloth, $2 50.

DESHLER'S AFTERNOONS WITH THE POETS.
Afternoons with the Poets. By C. D. DESHLER. 16mo, Cloth, $1 75.

ENGLISH MEN OF LETTERS. EDITED BY JOHN MORLEY.
12mo, Cloth, 75 cents a volume. PEOPLE'S EDITION. 36 vols. in 12. 16mo, Cloth, $12 00. (*Sold only in sets.*)

JOHNSON. By Leslie Stephen.—GIBBON. By J. C. Morison.—SCOTT. By R. H. Hutton.—SHELLEY. By John Addington Symonds.—HUME. By Professor Huxley.—GOLDSMITH. By William Black.—DEFOE. By William Minto.—BURNS. By Principal Shairp. SPENSER.—By Dean Church.—THACKERAY. By Anthony Trollope.—BURKE. By John Morley.—MILTON. By Mark Pattison.—SOUTHEY. By Edward Dowden.—CHAUCER. By Adolphus William Ward.—BUNYAN. By James Anthony Froude.—COWPER. By Goldwin Smith.—POPE. By Leslie Stephen.—BYRON. By John Nichol.—LOCKE. By Thomas Fowler.—WORDSWORTH. By F. W. H. Myers.—DRYDEN. By G. Saintsbury.—HAWTHORNE. By Henry James, Jr.—LANDOR. By Sidney Colvin.—DE QUINCEY. By David Masson.—LAMB. By Alfred Ainger. BENTLEY. By R. C. Jebb.—DICKENS. By A. W. Ward.—GRAY. By E. W. Gosse.—SWIFT. By Leslie Stephen.—STERNE. By H. D. Traill.—MACAULAY. By James Cotter Morison.—FIELDING. By Austin Dobson.—SHERIDAN. By Mrs. Oliphant.—ADDISON. By W. J. Courthope.—BACON. By R. W. Church, Dean of St. Paul's.—COLERIDGE. By H. D. Traill.—SIDNEY. By J. A. Symonds.—KEATS. By Sidney Colvin. (*Other volumes in preparation.*)

SOME ISSUES IN HARPER'S HALF-HOUR SERIES.
GOLDSMITH'S PLAYS. 32mo, Paper, 25 cents; Cloth, 40 cents.
GOLDSMITH'S POEMS. 32mo, Paper, 20 cents; Cloth, 35 cents.
SHERIDAN'S PLAYS.
  THE RIVALS and THE SCHOOL FOR SCANDAL. Comedies. By RICHARD BRINSLEY SHERIDAN. 32mo, Paper, 25 cents; Cloth, 40 cents.
COWPER'S TASK. A Poem in Six Books. By WILLIAM COWPER. 32mo, Paper, 20 cents; Cloth, 35 cents.
SIR WALTER SCOTT'S POEMS.
  THE LAY OF THE LAST MINSTREL. 32mo, Paper, 20 cents; Cloth, 35 cents.
  THE LADY OF THE LAKE. 32mo, Paper, 25 cents; Cloth, 40 cents.
  MARMION. 32mo, Paper, 25 cents; Cloth, 40 cents.
BALLADS OF BATTLE AND BRAVERY. Selected by W. G. M'CABE. 32mo, Paper, 25 cents; Cloth, 40 cents.
LITERATURE SERIES. By EUGENE LAWRENCE. In Seven Volumes. 32mo, Paper, 25 cents each; Cloth, 40 cents each.
  AMERICAN LITERATURE.—ENGLISH LITERATURE.—Romance Period.—Classical Period.—Modern Period.—MEDIÆVAL LITERATURE.—LATIN LITERATURE.—GREEK LITERATURE.
GERMAN LITERATURE. By HELEN S. CONANT. 32mo, Paper, 25 cents; Cloth, 40 cents.
SPANISH LITERATURE. By HELEN S. CONANT. 32mo, Paper, 25 cents; Cloth, 40 cents.

ENGLISH'S POETICAL WORKS.
  THE BOY'S BOOK OF BATTLE LYRICS. By THOMAS DUNN ENGLISH, M.D., LL.D. Illustrated. Square 8vo, Ornamental Cloth.
  AMERICAN BALLADS. By THOMAS DUNN ENGLISH, M.D., LL.D. 32mo, Paper, 25 cents; Cloth, 40 cents.

Selected Home Reading.

ILLUSTRATED BY E. A. ABBEY:
"THE QUIET LIFE." Certain Verses by Various Hands: the Motive set forth in a Prologue and Epilogue by AUSTIN DOBSON; the whole adorned with numerous drawings by EDWIN A. ABBEY and ALFRED PARSONS. 4to, Ornamental Leather, $7 50. (*In a Box*.)

OLD SONGS. Illustrated by EDWIN A. ABBEY, With Decorative Designs by ALFRED PARSONS. 4to, Ornamental Leather, 7 50. (*In a Box*.)

SHE STOOPS TO CONQUER, OR, THE MISTAKES OF A NIGHT. A Comedy. By Dr. GOLDSMITH. Illustrated by EDWIN A. ABBEY. With Ten Full-page Photo-gravure Reproductions, printed on separate plates, and numerous Wood-engravings. Folio, Illuminated Leather, Guilt Edges, $20 00. (*In a Box*.)

SELECTIONS FROM THE POEMS OF ROBERT HERRICK. With numerous Illustrations by EDWIN A. ABBEY. 4to, Illuminated Cloth, Gilt Edges, $7 50. (*In a Box*.)

ENGLISH LITERATURE IN THE EIGHTEENTH CENTURY.
By THOMAS SERGEANT PERRY. 12mo, Cloth, $2 00.

COLERIDGE'S ANCIENT MARINER. ILLUSTRATED BY DORÉ.
The Rime of the Ancient Mariner. By SAMUEL TAYLOR COLERIDGE. Illustrated by GUSTAV DORÉ. Folio, Cloth, $10 00.

POE'S RAVEN. ILLUSTRATED BY DORÉ.
The Raven. By EDGAR ALLAN POE. Illustrated by GUSTAV DORÉ. With Comment by E. C. STEDMAN. Folio (Uniform with Doré's *Ancient Mariner*), Illuminated Cloth, Gilt Edges, and in a neat Box, $10 00.

SYMONDS'S WORKS.
STUDIES OF THE GREEK POETS. By J. A. SYMONDS. Revised and Enlarged by the Author. In two Volumes. Square, 16mo, Cloth, $3 50.
SKETCHES AND STUDIES IN SOUTHERN EUROPE. By J. A. SYMONDS. In two Volumes. Post 8vo, Cloth, $4 00.

MAHAFFY'S GREEK LITERATURE.
A History of Classical Greek Literature. By J. P. MAHAFFY. 2 vols., 12mo, Cloth, $4 00.

SIMCOX'S LATIN LITERATURE.
A History of Latin Literature, from Ennius to Boethius. By GEORGE AUGUSTUS SIMCOX, M.A. In two Volumes. 12mo, Cloth, $4 00.

SONGS OF OUR YOUTH.
Set to Music. By Miss MULOCK. Square 4to, Cloth, $2 50.

OUR CHILDREN'S SONGS. ILLUSTRATED.
Selected and Arranged by the Rev. S. IRENÆUS Prime, D.D. 8vo, Cloth, $1 00.

BAYNE'S LESSONS FROM MY MASTERS.
Lessons from My Masters: Carlyle, Tennyson, and Ruskin. By PETER BAYNE, M.A., LL.D. 12mo, Cloth, $1 75.

PUBLISHED BY HARPER & BROTHERS, NEW YORK.

☞ HARPER & BROTHERS *will send any of the foregoing works by mail, postage prepaid, to any part of the United States, Canada, or Mexico, on receipt of the price.*

Printed in Dunstable, United Kingdom